AF705547

How to Retire

Retire Knowing You Will Enjoy Every Day

Steven Scanlan

Copyright

HOW TO RETIRE

First Published in Chemainus, Vancouver Island, 2025

ISBN: 978-1-989681-45-9

Text and Graphics, Copyright © Steven Scanlan, 2025. All rights reserved.

A Catalogue entry for the title and name of this book reside with the Canadian Registry of ISBN.

No part of this publication, in whole or in part, may be copied, reproduced, republished, uploaded, posted, transmitted, stored in a retrieval system, or otherwise distributed by any means or in any form, whether electronic, mechanical, photocopying, recording, scanning, or otherwise, without the prior express written permission of Steven Scanlan.

This prohibition expressly includes, without limitation, the use of any content, data, text, or other material contained herein for purposes of training or enhancing artificial intelligence (AI) models or systems; inclusion in any AI or machine learning datasets, language models, knowledge graphs, or neural networks; or integration into any automated retrieval, storage, or generative systems.

Unauthorised use, reproduction, or distribution of this material, including but not limited to scraping, mining, or indexing for commercial, research, academic, or AI training purposes, constitutes a violation of applicable intellectual property laws and may result in legal action.

To obtain permission for use, reproduction, or licensing, please contact Steven Scanlan directly in writing.

Table of Contents

Foreword

It happens quietly, like a tap on the shoulder in a crowded room. One day, you're immersed in the routine of work, promotions, paychecks, and packed calendars, and then, the question appears: “Am I ready for retirement?”

Some hear the question of retirement in their thirties, triggered by a late-night article about pensions and compound interest. Others hear it in their fifties, startled by a colleague’s retirement announcement and the realisation that the clock is ticking.

For a few, it doesn't hit until the final work anniversary party has ended, and by then, panic may have replaced planning.

This book is for everyone considering the prospect of retirement or who are already in the process of being retired.

Introduction

Welcome to the wonderful world of retirement: A journey from "What now?" to "This is great!"

You've retired! No more early morning alarms, no more endless emails, no more pretending to understand the latest office jargon. Freedom at last! But wait... what are you supposed to do with all this time on your hands?

The truth is, while retirement is often painted as a golden age of leisure and relaxation, the reality can be a bit different. Sure, you've got all this newfound freedom, but sometimes it feels like you've been handed the keys to an empty castle. What exactly are you supposed to do with it? The challenge isn't having too little to do; it's having too much time to fill.

You might have thought the day you'd retire would be filled with sunrises on the beach, long walks through the golf course, and leisurely lunches with friends. Instead, you find yourself staring at the clock, wondering where the hours have gone. And let's face it, unless you're a professional napper or a championship level couch-potato, having an excess of time on your hands can sometimes be the biggest obstacle to enjoying your retirement.

You're not alone. Many people face this very dilemma. In fact, it's not uncommon for retirees to feel a little lost after their career ends. Even if you retired by choice, after a few decades of gruelling work, you might find that your brain starts searching for a new purpose. It's like that moment when your phone gets a software update and you're left wondering, "What the heck was wrong with the old version?"

It's a bit of an adjustment. But don't worry, this isn't the beginning of a sad, aimless existence. Far from it! You've just entered the world of endless possibilities.

Our Story - My Own Retirement

Let's talk about how I treated the move to retirement. The company, bless its heart, decided it was time to "restructure" (aka, "Let's shake things up and see who falls out"). It didn't surprise me when I was shown the door. Honestly, I was kind of waiting for it.

During the latter part of my career, I was reassigned from my role as Quality Director, a position in which I was highly competent and experienced, to a role I neither desired nor was qualified for. Despite my repeated warnings, management proceeded with these changes. This decision exemplifies what has become known as the Peter Principle (Peter, Hull, 1969, Harper,) which asserts that employees in hierarchical organisations are often promoted, or reassigned, beyond their level of competence. In my case, I was not elevated, but displaced into roles misaligned with my skills, and crucially, never returned to a role I was proficient in. The company failed to recognise the misstep, leaving me in a position where I could not contribute effectively. Ultimately, this led to my premature retirement. I have no hard feelings. The whole thing was inevitable. The universe has a funny way of nudging you in the direction of change, even when you're quite comfortable sitting in your well-worn chair of routine. After all, who doesn't love a little spontaneous shake-up? (Okay, maybe not everyone. But that's the nature of retirement, it's full of surprises, some of them not entirely pleasant.)

Now that I had all this free time, an entire 37.5 to 60 hours a week to fill, I was faced with a choice: I could either spend my days wandering aimlessly around the house, looking for things to do, or I could embrace this new phase and make it my own. Spoiler alert: I chose the latter. But it took some trial and error. A lot of "what should I do now?" moments. And guess what? That'sone of the reasons I wrote this book. To guide us all through the often confusing yet exhilarating world of retirement time management.

Let's address the elephant in the room. You've got a lot of time now. And yes, it's true that too much time can become an issue. At first, you might feel like you've won the lottery. You wake up when you want, go to bed when you want, and if you want to wear sweatpants all day, well, that's your business. However, after a few weeks of unstructured time, it's common for retirees to start experiencing what I like to call "too much time syndrome." It's a real condition, and the symptoms can include aimless wandering, an excessive number of cups of coffee, and an almost pathological need to reorganise your bookshelf.

You might have the best intentions at first. "I'm going to start a new hobby! I'll learn how to paint! I'll finally take up knitting!" But, as the days stretch on, you start to realise that knitting might not be as thrilling as you thought it would be. And the painting? Well, let's just say the canvas is still gathering dust. You're not alone. Many retirees go through a phase of trying to figure out *what* they should be doing with all this time, and whether what they're doing is enough.

So, how do you go from feeling overwhelmed by time to feeling fulfilled and content in your retirement? The answer is surprisingly simple: structure. But before you roll your eyes and mutter, "I left the corporate grind for freedom, not another schedule," let me assure you: structuring your time doesn't mean putting yourself in prison of obligations. It means finding a balance between leisure and purpose, between relaxation and activity.

First, let's talk about purpose. You've had a job for a long time. Maybe decades. That job, while sometimes frustrating, probably gave you a sense of purpose. Whether you were solving problems, creating things, or simply keeping the ship afloat, your work gave you direction. When you retire, you need to find a new form of purpose.

That doesn't mean you need to volunteer for every cause under the sun (though, if that's your thing, more power to you.) Purpose can come from small, everyday actions. Maybe you take up a hobby you've always wanted to try, like photography, pottery or gardening. Maybe you decide to take on a new project, like writing a book (ahem, no pressure). The point is, without purpose, you might find that the days start to feel a bit empty. And trust me, you don't want that.

Next, let's talk about pacing. Retirement isn't a race. You don't have to fill every single hour with something productive. It's okay to do nothing sometimes.

Seriously. You've earned it. But if you're finding that "doing nothing" is starting to feel a little too much like "doing nothing with no end in sight," it might be time to shake things up a little. Set aside some time each week to tackle a project, maybe something creative or something practical. Something to engage your mind and get you excited. Just don't feel pressured to be constantly busy. Slow and steady wins the retirement race.

At the end of the day, retirement is all about you. It's a time to rediscover what excites you, what brings you joy, and what makes you feel like you're still contributing to the world in some way. Whether that means traveling the world, learning a new skill, writing your memoir, volunteering, or simply enjoying long coffee mornings with friends, it's up to you.

One thing that's crucial to remember is this: retirement doesn't have to be perfect. You don't need to have a meticulously planned day with scheduled activities, exercise routines, and a 3-course lunch menu every day. Some days, it's perfectly fine to just enjoy a cup of tea while reading a good book. Other days, you might feel the urge to run a marathon or take a pottery class. Whatever you do, just make sure that it's something that feels right for you.

It's also essential to remember that retirement is an evolving process. You don't have to have everything figured out on day one (or even year one). The beauty of retirement is that it gives you the freedom to experiment and discover new things about yourself. You'll likely go through different phases, maybe you'll start out with a burst of energy, only to find yourself in a "I'm going to watch all the Netflix" phase. But that's okay! The key is to stay curious, be patient with yourself, and keep looking for ways to make this new chapter of life fulfilling.

You will quickly learn, retirement isn't just about filling time; it's about making time work for YOU. Embrace it. Own it. Plan for it, but don't stress over it. Fill your days with things that bring you joy, challenge you, or simply make you laugh. The fact is, you've earned this time, so make it count in your own way.

After all, retirement is the only time in your life when you get to be the CEO of your own schedule. No more meetings you don't want to attend, no more inboxes you must respond to immediately. Just you, your time, and endless possibilities.

So, what are you going to do with all that time?

Over the following chapters we will look at how you can plan your retirement, examine how you will be impacted by the change and identify opportunities to enjoy the time available to you.

Retirement Isn't a Destination, It's a Transition

For generations, we were taught to view retirement as a finish line: the golden years, the end of work, the reward for decades of effort. But retirement isn't an end. It's a massive life transition. One that reshapes not just your finances, but your identity, your daily structure, your relationships, your health, and your sense of purpose.

Imagine it. For 30 or 40 years, your life has revolved around work. You've had goals tied to promotions, salaries, projects, and deadlines. You've measured your time in meetings, vacations, and paydays. And then, suddenly, all that changes. You have time. But do you have direction? You have freedom. But do you have a plan?

Retirement is not a permanent vacation. It's the start of a new chapter, one that requires its own blueprint. Without a clear vision and strategy, that new chapter can become one of uncertainty, regret, or even financial stress. But with the right tools and mindset, retirement can be your most fulfilling and empowered season of life.

Retirement Planning Is a Skill

The idea of retirement planning can seem overwhelming. Investments, insurance, taxes, healthcare, these are big, complicated topics. But here's the truth: Retirement planning isn't magic. It's strategy. And like any good strategy, it can be broken down into understandable parts, learned at your own pace, and customised to your needs.

You don't need to be a financial wizard to retire well. You just need clarity, intention, and action.

The Five Pillars of Retirement Planning

Over the course of this book, we'll explore five foundational pillars that support a successful retirement:

1. **Vision** – What does your ideal retirement look like? (Hint: It's different for everyone.)
2. **Money** – How much will you need, and where will it come from?
3. **Health** – How will you prepare for medical costs, aging, and maintaining quality of life?
4. **Purpose** – What will give your life meaning once the office, job title, and routine are gone?
5. **Legacy** – What do you want to leave behind, financially, emotionally, and ethically?

Each pillar matters. Each one influences the others. Focus only on the money, and you may find yourself financially secure but emotionally adrift. Focus only on purpose, and you may have rich days but strained resources. Retirement isn't about extremes, it's about balance.

A Real Story: Why Planning Matters

I met a man named Bill in my wife's small shop on Vancouver Island. Bill was 64, cheerful, energetic, and gearing up to retire within a year. When I asked if he had a retirement plan, he gave me a confident grin. "Of course," he said. "I'll golf, travel, maybe fix up the old car."

It sounded great. But when we looked closer, the gaps were obvious. He hadn't budgeted for healthcare costs beyond age 65. He underestimated the tax burden on his pension income. He hadn't considered inflation, and he had no plan for long-term care.

What Bill had, wasn't a plan, it was a dream. A good dream, but one that lacked structure.

Fortunately, Bill faced reality in time. He postponed retirement for a few years, adjusted his savings, and educated himself. By the time he turned 67, he had what he needed: a workable plan, a solid income stream, and peace of mind. He even sent me a photo of that beautifully restored car.

Planning didn't make Bill wealthy. It gave him options. It gave him confidence. And that's the true power of your retirement strategy.

The Emotional Shift

Retirement is often described in numbers. But beneath those numbers is something more human: identity.

For many people, especially those with long careers, work becomes a core part of who they are. When that ends, it can create a crisis of identity. "Who am I now?" is a question many new retirees face, sometimes with more fear than freedom.

This emotional shift is real. That's why retirement planning must include more than RRSPs, IRAs, or pensions. It must include your values, your goals, your personal development.

- What do you want your mornings to look like?
- What passions or hobbies have you put on hold?

- What contributions do you still want to make, to your family, your community, or the world?

Beyond the Basics

Let's expand the scope of your planning with a few often-overlooked components:

1. Longevity Planning

People are living longer than ever. If you retire at 65, you may need income for 25-30 more years. That makes retirement a decades-long financial phase, not a short break. Plan accordingly.

2. Housing Decisions

Will you downsize, age in place, move closer to family, or relocate for climate and cost? Housing is one of the most significant decisions that affects both lifestyle and budget.

3. Flexible Work or Entrepreneurship

Many retirees work part-time, consult, or start small businesses. Not out of necessity, but for purpose and connection. Flexible work can boost your income and your sense of identity.

4. Technology and Digital Literacy

Technology isn't just for the young. Mastering online banking, telehealth, and social media can keep you connected, safe, and independent.

5. Social Connection Planning

Isolation is a major risk in retirement. Build and maintain a network. Friendships, clubs, volunteering, and family ties help ensure your emotional well-being.

Your Retirement Planning Starts Today

By picking up this book, you've already taken the first step: awareness. Whether you're 30 or 60, whether you earn six figures or you're just getting by, retirement planning starts the moment you commit to making it a priority.

Think of it like building a house. You need a vision, a blueprint, the right tools, and the willingness to do the work. But the reward is worth it: stability, freedom, fulfilment, and peace of mind.

In the pages ahead, we'll dive deeper. We'll talk numbers, timelines, accounts, and strategies. But we'll also explore meaning, passion, and how to design a retirement that feels as good as it looks on paper.

So, take a deep breath, grab a pen, and let's begin building your next chapter, on your terms, and with purpose.

Our Story - Our Retirement Planning

For most of our working lives, retirement felt like a distant, almost abstract concept. My wife and I were in our late 50s, 58 to be exact, before we seriously considered what retirement might actually look like. Until then, we had always assumed there would be time. But time, as we learned, has a way of sneaking up on you.

It wasn't until we took a hard look at our financial situation that reality set in. The mortgage still had years left on it, and we had a handful of credit cards with balances we'd been meaning to pay down "one of these days." Suddenly, "one of these days" had a deadline. With less than a decade left before I turned 67, the age we initially targeted for retirement, we realised we had to act, and quickly.

So we got to work. We approached the challenge with renewed energy, reviewing every aspect of our financial life. We mapped out our income, trimmed our expenses, and created a plan with the goal of entering retirement debt-free. It felt good to take control. We set clear milestones: eliminate credit card debt, reduce discretionary spending, and most critically, chip away at that mortgage.

But, as I mentioned in the previous chapter, life has a way of surprising you. Circumstances, some expected ,others not, shifted our plans. In the end, we chose to retire earlier than we'd intended, before all our financial goals were fully met. And here's the truth: we don't regret it.

Sure, we still carry a small mortgage, and no, the plan didn't unfold exactly as we had envisioned. But the decision to retire when we did felt right. It was right. Retirement, we learned, is not just about numbers, it's also about timing, health, opportunity, and the courage to say, "This is the Time."

We didn't just plan for finances; we planned for life. Our revised retirement plans included long-delayed dreams: taking an extended vacation, finishing the basement (a project always shelved for "next year"), and even returning to university, something I'd long wanted but never prioritised.

Now, we find ourselves living a slightly altered version of the plan, and truthfully, it's working. It's not perfect, and we had to let go of some ideals, but it suits us. We're learning, traveling, and finally doing the things we put off during our working years.

If there's one lesson I can share from this journey, it's this: start planning earlier than we did.

> It's never too late to take control and redefine what your retirement can be.

Retirement Transition Checklist

Use this checklist to assess your readiness for the emotional, financial, and lifestyle shifts retirement brings. Put a tick in the corresponding box, if you agree with the statement.

Vision & Lifestyle

- ☐ I have a clear picture of what my ideal retirement looks like (daily routines, hobbies, travel, etc.).
- ☐ I've discussed my retirement plans with my partner or family.
- ☐ I know where I want to live during retirement and have explored housing options.
- ☐ I have a plan for how I'll stay socially connected and avoid isolation.
- ☐ I've identified hobbies, volunteer work, or projects that excite me.

Financial Readiness

- ☐ I know how much I need to retire comfortably (monthly/yearly).
- ☐ I've reviewed all my income sources (pension, savings, CPP/OAS, RRSPs, IRAs, annuities, etc.).
- ☐ I've created or updated a retirement budget.
- ☐ I've accounted for inflation in my long-term planning.
- ☐ I've considered the tax implications of my retirement income.

- ☐ I have a withdrawal strategy for my retirement accounts.
- ☐ I've planned for emergency expenses or unexpected costs.

Health & Longevity

- ☐ I understand my health insurance coverage before and after 65.
- ☐ I've factored future healthcare costs (prescriptions, dental, vision, etc.) into my plan.
- ☐ I have a plan for long-term care (insurance, savings, or support options).
- ☐ I engage in regular physical activity and monitor my health.
- ☐ I've identified preferred medical professionals or specialists in my area.

Purpose & Identity

- ☐ I've considered how retirement will affect my sense of identity and self-worth.
- ☐ I've explored opportunities for giving back (mentorship, community work, causes I care about).
- ☐ I'm learning new things or working on personal development goals.
- ☐ I have a plan for how to stay mentally and emotionally engaged.

Legacy & Estate Planning

- ☐ I have an updated will and designated power of attorney.

- ☐ I've discussed my wishes with my family or executor.
- ☐ I've organised and documented important financial and legal information.
- ☐ I have an estate plan that reflects my values and goals.
- ☐ I've considered charitable giving or legacy contributions.

Technology & Preparedness

- ☐ I'm comfortable using online banking and financial tools.
- ☐ I can access telehealth or virtual medical services.
- ☐ I use technology to stay connected with family and friends.

Scoring:

If you've checked fewer than 10 items, it may be time to slow down and revisit some key areas.

If you've checked 10–20, you're making progress, keep going!

If you've checked more than 20, you're on the path to a confident, intentional retirement transition.

When Is the Best Time to Retire?

There's a popular myth that retirement happens at 65, like turning the page of a calendar, you hit the magic number and suddenly it's time to sail off into the sunset. There is no one-size-fits-all retirement age.

The "best" time to retire is deeply personal. It depends on your finances, your health, your lifestyle goals, your expenditure, your family circumstances, and your personality.

Let's explore the key factors that will help you define your best time to retire.

1. The Financial Readiness Test

Before anything else, ask yourself: Can I afford to stop working?

Retirement isn't about hitting an age; it's about reaching a level of financial independence where your assets and income streams can support your lifestyle without a paycheck.

Here's a basic financial readiness checklist:

- Have you calculated your annual retirement expenses?
- Do you have at least 25–30 times your expected annual spending saved or invested? (This is the general rule of thumb for a safe withdrawal rate of 3–4%.)

- Will your income streams, such as Social Security, pensions, annuities, rental income, or investment withdrawals, cover your needs for potentially 30+ years?
- Have you accounted for inflation, taxes, and rising healthcare costs?
- Do you have an emergency fund or safety net in place?

If the answer to any of these is no or uncertain, it may not be time to retire yet. But don't worry, we'll walk through how to build up those numbers in later chapters.

2. The Social Security Timing Game

Social Security is one of the most misunderstood pieces of the retirement puzzle. You can start claiming benefits as early as age 62 (depending on the country), but that comes with a catch: your monthly benefit will be permanently reduced compared to waiting until your Full Retirement Age (FRA), typically between 66 and 67, depending on your birth year.

Wait until age 70, and you'll receive the maximum possible monthly benefit, up to 30% more than at FRA and 75% more than at age 62.

So, when's the best time to start claiming? It depends:

- If you need the income, claiming early may be necessary.
- If you're in poor health or have a lower life expectancy, taking benefits earlier might make sense.

- If you have strong longevity in your family and other income sources to delay, waiting can significantly boost your lifetime benefits.

The key is to run the numbers and make an informed decision, not just grab benefits the moment you're eligible.

3. The Emotional and Psychological Factor

Believe it or not, not everyone is emotionally ready to retire. Some people retire too early and feel lost. Others work longer than necessary, clinging to structure and identity.

Ask yourself:

- Do you enjoy your work, or are you counting the minutes until it's over?
- Have you envisioned what your days will look like in retirement?
- Do you have hobbies, relationships, or passions that will fill your time and give you a sense of purpose?
- Have you and your spouse or partner talked about what retirement will look like for both of you?
- Retirement isn't just about quitting work; it's about moving toward something meaningful. Those who retire with no plan beyond "not working" often experience boredom, depression, or regret.

4. Health and Longevity Considerations

Health plays a major role in deciding when to retire. For some, medical issues force an early exit from the workforce. For others, good health enables them to work, and enjoy retirement, well into their 70s or 80s.

Here are a few key questions:

- Are you physically and mentally capable of continuing to work?
- If you live in the USA decide if you will be covered by health insurance if you retire, before becoming eligible for Medicare at age 65?
- Are you mentally prepared to shift from active work life to a more relaxed pace?
- Have you planned for long-term care or assisted living in your later years?

Retiring early without health coverage or a long-term care plan is one of the most expensive mistakes retirees make.

5. Timing Around Market Conditions

Sometimes, life makes the decision for you.

You might delay retirement during a market downturn to avoid withdrawing investments at a loss. Or you might accelerate your timeline to care for a loved one, escape burnout, or relocate with a spouse.

Life is not a straight path, and your retirement date may need to adjust based on:

- Economic conditions
- Career transitions

- Family health
- Opportunities for travel or volunteering
- Grandchildren or other family commitments

Being flexible is a sign of wise planning.

So… When Is the Right Time?

Here's the truth: The best time to retire is when three things align:

1. **You are financially ready** - you have enough savings or income to support your lifestyle.
2. **You are emotionally ready** - you have a plan, a purpose, and a support system in place.
3. **You are medically and logistically ready** - your health, insurance, and timing make sense for your unique life.

For some, this may be age 55. For others, it's 70. There's no "wrong" answer, only your answer.

Case Studies

- **Mark, age 58** – Retired early after selling his business. He travels six months a year and consults part-time for fun. His success came from planning aggressively in his 40s.
- **Linda, age 66** – Retired at full retirement age, collecting a full Social Security benefit. She volunteers weekly and helps raise her grandchildren. She waited to ensure her mortgage was paid off.

- **George, age 72** – Still working. He loves his job and doesn't need the money but enjoys mentoring younger colleagues. He delayed Social Security and has maximised his benefits.

Each of them made the right decision, because they made their decision, based on preparation and personal priorities.

Our Story - My Own Retirement

Retirement planning often unfolds in one of two ways: you either walk steadily toward it on your own terms, or it arrives unexpectedly, demanding you rethink everything. For me, it was a bit of both.

My wife and I had spent three months discussing retirement. We were methodical, even cautious. Using the reflective questionnaire outlined earlier in this book, we evaluated our values, our lifestyle needs, and our long-term goals. Together, we set a target date three years into the future. That timeline seemed realistic and safe, enough time to prepare financially, mentally, and emotionally.

But here's the truth: those three years stretched ahead of me like a long corridor with no windows. I was still working under the weight of deadlines I didn't choose, attending meetings that drained rather than inspired, and watching someone else set the pace and purpose of my life. I told myself, "Just three more years," as if freedom was something I had to earn by enduring.

Then life surprised me. One afternoon, I received an unexpected invitation to a virtual meeting with my manager. Joining us was a third person I didn't recognise. Without preamble, my manager introduced them as a representative from Human Resources and promptly exited the call. In the next few minutes, my world shifted. My role was being restructured, I was told. My services were no longer required. In less diplomatic terms, I was being let go.

It was a surreal moment. Not the retirement I had envisioned. Not the send-off I'd imagined. Yet, what followed taught me something crucial about how retirement, and life, actually works.

As part of my severance, I received a settlement that allowed us to clear our remaining debts. That moment of financial clarity gave us pause. My wife and I looked at each other and asked a powerful question: What if this isn't the end, but the beginning?

We sat down, not to set a far-off goal, but to assess our present reality. We opened spreadsheets, rechecked our pension balances, reviewed our expenses, and calculated a realistic monthly budget. It wasn't lavish, but it was workable. More importantly, it was ours to shape.

And so, I stepped into retirement. Not as a defeated employee, but as someone finally unbound. In many ways, that unplanned exit from my career became the most liberating moment of my adult life. The door that closed so suddenly made room for the one I didn't know I was ready to walk through.

Since then, I've become an author, sharing what I've learned about this stage of life. Not because I planned it that way, but because retirement, especially early or unexpected retirement, isn't an end. It's a shift. A reframing. A reawakening of identity, purpose, and possibility.

Next Step: Define Your Retirement Timeline

At the end of this chapter, take a moment to reflect:

- What age do you want to retire?
- What age can you afford to retire?
- What would have to happen in your life to align those two?

Remember: The goal isn't just to retire. It's to retire well.

Retirement Income Needs

Retirement may seem like a distant dream for many people, but when the time comes to transition out of the workforce, it can feel overwhelming if you haven't properly planned. One of the most crucial aspects of retirement planning is understanding how much income you'll need to cover your living expenses, both basic and discretionary.

Whether you're nearing retirement or decades away, it's never too early, or too late, to start planning. This guide is applicable across the Western world, from the U.S. and Canada to the U.K. and Australia. While retirement systems and costs of living may differ slightly from country to country, the principles of planning for retirement income remain universal.

1. Understanding Your Retirement Income Needs

At the core of retirement planning lies one simple question: How much income will you need to live on once you're no longer earning a paycheck? Your retirement income needs are determined by your expected lifestyle, the costs of maintaining it, and how long you expect to live.

But the reality of retirement income goes beyond the basics. Many retirees desire more than just the ability to pay bills, they want to maintain a certain standard of living, pursue hobbies, travel, or even take on new ventures. These factors will all influence the amount of income you'll need in retirement.

Key Considerations:

- **Living Expenses:** These are the day-to-day costs of running your household, rent or mortgage, utilities, groceries, transportation, and insurance.
- **Healthcare Costs:** As you age, healthcare becomes an increasingly important factor. Medical insurance premiums, out-of-pocket costs, and prescription medication can add up.
- **Inflation:** The purchasing power of money declines over time due to inflation. Even a modest 2% annual inflation rate can significantly impact your cost of living over a couple of decades.
- **Lifestyle Choices:** These expenses include things like entertainment, dining out, travel, and hobbies. Many people have aspirations for a more active and fulfilling retirement, but these activities come at a cost.
- **Debt:** Existing debts, including mortgages, car loans, student loans, or credit card balances, must be factored in when estimating your future needs. Carrying debt into retirement can be a significant drain on your income.
- **Taxes:** Depending on your sources of income, taxes in retirement may differ from your working years. It's essential to factor in how pensions, social security benefits, investment income, and other sources will be taxed.

2. Estimating Your Annual Retirement Expenses

Before calculating how much money you'll need to save for retirement, you need to understand how much you'll spend once you retire. A common method of estimating your future retirement expenses is to begin by evaluating your current spending.

Step 1: Track Your Current Spending

For at least a few months, preferably a year, track every cent you spend. This can be done manually through a spreadsheet, or with the help of apps like Mint, YNAB (You Need a Budget), or even your bank's built-in tracking tools.

Categorise your expenses into two main buckets:

- **Essential Expenses:** These include necessities such as:
    - Housing (mortgage, rent, property taxes, etc.)
    - Utilities (electricity, gas, water, internet, etc.)
    - Food and groceries
    - Transportation (car payments, fuel, public transport)
    - Insurance premiums (health, home, car, etc.)
    - Taxes

- **Discretionary Expenses:** These are non-essential but may include:
    - Dining out and entertainment
    - Travel and vacations
    - Hobbies, fitness, and personal interests
    - Gifts and charity donations
    - Subscriptions (magazines, streaming services, etc.)

By categorising your expenses, you can get a sense of what you are currently spending, and more importantly, what you might be able to reduce or increase once retired.

Step 2: Estimate Future Changes

After tracking your current expenses, think about how they might change once you retire. Some costs may decrease, while others could increase.

- **Housing:** Will you still have a mortgage? Many people downsize in retirement, which could reduce housing costs. However, in some cases, housing expenses may remain constant, or you might choose to move to a more expensive location.
- **Transportation:** Will you still need to commute to work? If so, you might save on gas, public transport, or car maintenance. However, you might also travel more often for leisure in retirement, increasing transportation costs.
- **Healthcare:** Healthcare costs tend to rise as people age. Depending on where you live, healthcare costs may become a significant portion of your expenses, particularly if you are in a country that requires private insurance or out-of-pocket costs for healthcare, dental, or prescription services.
- **Discretionary Expenses:** Are you planning on traveling more? Will you spend more on hobbies, fitness, or other personal interests? Many people look forward to having more time for leisure activities in retirement, and this could lead to higher spending on these areas.

Step 3: Account for Inflation

Inflation is an important factor when estimating your retirement expenses. Over time, the cost of goods and services tends to rise. Historically, inflation in Western economies has averaged around 2-3% per year.

For example, if you estimate that you will need $40,000 per year in retirement, you'll need to account for inflation to ensure that amount remains sufficient. If inflation averages 2% per year, $40,000 in 30 years will be worth much less than it is today.

You can calculate the impact of inflation using the following formula:

Future Value=Present Value×(1+Inflation Rate)Yea rsFuture\ Value = Present\ Value \times (1 + Inflation\ Rate)^{Years}

So, if you expect to retire in 30 years and need $40,000 a year in today's dollars, the amount you'll need in 30 years, with 2% inflation, is:

Future Value=40,000×(1+0.02)30=40,000×1.8114= 72,456Future\ Value = 40,000 \times (1 + 0.02)^{30} = 40,000 \times 1.8114 = 72,456

This means that in 30 years, you will need $72,456 per year to maintain the same purchasing power that $40,000 offers today.

Our Story - Retirement Finances

If there's one question that keeps almost every soon-to-be retiree awake at night, it's this: Can I afford to retire?

That was certainly the case for us. The emotional shift of leaving work is profound, but it's the financial uncertainty that can truly shake your confidence.

When retirement unexpectedly arrived on our doorstep, we were forced to answer this question head-on. The first step we took was simple, but critical. We gathered all the facts.

We listed our expected sources of income, pensions, government benefits, and a small settlement. We then did what every financial planner recommends but few of us actually enjoy doing: we tallied our monthly expenses with brutal honesty. Groceries, utilities, transportation, insurance, home maintenance, entertainment, dental care, everything went into the spreadsheet. We even included "surprise" expenses, because in retirement, surprises don't come with a salary to cushion them.

Once we had the numbers in front of us, we applied a well-known concept I call the **80% Rule**, outlined in Rule 3 below. This rule assumes that certain work-related costs, like commuting, work wardrobe updates, and daily coffees, will naturally disappear. For us, the 80% benchmark became a guiding light. If we could meet our needs and maintain a decent quality of life on that reduced income, we felt we were on solid ground.

The good news? Our numbers worked. I could retire. The caveat? We had to shift our habits.

While I was working, my wife and I dined out twice a week, usually without a second thought. It was routine, even relaxing. In retirement, we decided to reserve dining out for special occasions. Now, we go out once a month, and when we do, it feels celebratory again.

We also scaled back on travel. While previously we might book a spontaneous weekend away or a big international holiday every year, retirement demanded a different rhythm. Now, we plan travel carefully, with a keen eye on value. And honestly, we find joy in smaller, slower experiences, a road trip along the coast, a visit to family, a quiet cabin in the woods.

Discretionary spending, things like clothes, gifts, hobbies, or gadgets, also saw a noticeable reduction. We gave ourselves monthly allowances for personal spending.

Some costs, however, didn't change. We both still drive, so transportation remains a significant line in the budget. Fuel, maintenance, insurance, it all adds up. We decided to keep both vehicles for now, recognising the independence and flexibility they provide. But this may evolve as our needs change.

We also carry a small mortgage. While not ideal, we factored it into our monthly budget and planned to pay it down aggressively over the coming years. Every retirement budget looks different, yours might include rent, condo fees, or perhaps you're mortgage-free. The key is knowing what your fixed costs are and planning around them.

Living in Canada, we're fortunate to have healthcare coverage for most medical needs. Still, dental and vision care remain out-of-pocket expenses. To prepare for those inevitable costs, new glasses, a crown, a root canal, we set aside a small sum each month into an "unexpected health" fund. It's a small buffer, but it prevents stress when those expenses inevitably pop up.

So, how do we feel now? We are by no means wealthy, but we're not struggling. We eat well. We stay active. We laugh. We see friends. We travel. Life didn't end; it simply changed. And that change brought with it a sense of control we hadn't felt in years. It's a new kind of freedom: freedom within limits.

If you're reading this and still unsure about your own numbers, my advice is simple: run them. Don't guess. Don't wait. Don't put it off until "next year." The moment you confront your financial reality is the moment you gain power over it. Whether your retirement is five years away or already underway, it's never too late to take control of your financial story.

3. The 80% Rule: A Common Guideline

A common rule of thumb to calculate your needs in retirement, is the 80% Rule, which suggests that most people will need about 80% of their pre-retirement income to maintain their lifestyle in retirement.

For example, if you currently earn $60,000 per year, the 80% Rule suggests that you'll need about $48,000 per year in retirement.

Why the 80% Rule Works (and When It Doesn't)

The idea behind the 80% Rule is that some expenses, particularly work-related expenses, will decrease when you retire. You might no longer need to buy work clothes, pay for commuting, or contribute to retirement savings, for example. However, the 80% Rule is a broad guideline, and your personal circumstances may cause it to be higher or lower.

When the 80% Rule Might Be Too Low:

- **Healthcare Costs:** If you live in a country without universal healthcare or if you have pre-existing medical conditions, or dental needs, healthcare costs can be a significant burden.
- **Debt:** If you have a mortgage, car payments, or other significant debt, you may need more than 80% of your pre-retirement income to pay off your obligations.
- **Travel and Leisure:** If you plan to travel frequently or engage in expensive hobbies in retirement, your lifestyle may require more than 80% of your current income.

When the 80% Rule Might Be Too High:

- **Downsizing or Relocating:** If you plan to downsize your home, move to a less expensive location, or significantly reduce discretionary spending, you may need less than 80% of your pre-retirement income.

4. The Four Percent Rule

Once you've estimated how much you'll need each year in retirement, the next step is figuring out how much to save to generate that income. One popular approach to this is the Four Percent Rule.

The Four Percent Rule suggests that if you have enough savings to generate 4% of your initial nest egg each year, your money will last for about 30 years. This strategy is based on historical returns from a diversified investment portfolio (stocks, bonds, etc.).

To calculate how much you need to save using the Four Percent Rule:

a) **Estimate Your Annual Retirement Expenses:** For example, let's say you've calculated you'll need $50,000 per year to cover all expenses.

b) **Multiply Your Annual Expenses by 25:** Using the Four Percent Rule, multiply your annual expenses by 25 to determine how much you need in savings. 50,000×25=1,250,00050,000 \times 25 = 1,250,000

This means that you would need approximately $1.25 million in savings to generate $50,000 per year using the Four Percent Rule.

While the Four Percent Rule is a helpful guide, it's not foolproof. Factors like market volatility, changes in living expenses, and inflation can affect how long your savings last.

5. Other Retirement Income Sources

In addition to savings, there are other income sources you may have access to in retirement, including:

- **Government Pensions/Social Security:** Depending on where you live, government pensions or social security programs can be a significant source of retirement income. The amount will vary based on your work history, contributions, and the country's policies.
- **Employer Pension Plans:** If you've worked for a company that offers a pension or retirement plan (such as a 401(k) in the U.S., or a superannuation

plan in Australia), this can provide a steady stream of income in retirement.

- **Investment Income:** Dividends from stocks, interest from bonds, or rental income from real estate investments can contribute to your retirement income.
- **Annuities:** Some retirees choose to purchase an annuity, which guarantees fixed payments for a certain number of years or for life.

6. Conclusion

Calculating your retirement income needs is a crucial step in ensuring you can live comfortably once you stop working. By carefully assessing your living expenses, estimating future costs, and applying rules like the 80% Rule and Four Percent Rule, you can determine how much you need to save and how much you'll need to generate annually.

Remember, these guidelines are just that, guidelines. Your specific circumstances, goals, and priorities will dictate how much you'll need in retirement. Planning, being flexible, and regularly revisiting your financial strategy will help you create a sustainable retirement plan. With careful thought and disciplined saving, you can enter retirement with peace of mind, knowing you've done the work to secure your future.

Remember – Finances provide you comfort, but Purpose gives you a reason to get up in the morning.

Hidden Retirement Dangers

Most people think retirement is simply about saving enough money and then riding off into the sunset. Unfortunately, this mindset can lead people straight into traps that threaten their financial well-being and the lifestyle they've worked so hard to build.

Even the most disciplined savers, those who contribute regularly to pensions, set budgets, and carefully plan their retirement dates, are often blindsided by hidden dangers that can derail their dreams for the future.

Whether you live in North America, Europe, Asia, or anywhere in between, these pitfalls can manifest in similar ways. In many countries, the idea that retirement will be a time to relax and enjoy life is challenged by unexpected financial or psychological hurdles. This chapter aims to shed light on those hidden dangers so that you can take proactive steps to avoid them, ensuring that you enter retirement with confidence and security.

1. Underestimating Longevity

The first, and most common, retirement mistake is underestimating how long you will live after you retire. Thanks to modern medicine and improved living standards, it's entirely possible that your retirement will last 30, 35, or even 40 years. If you retire at 60 and live until 95, you might need to fund nearly four decades of retirement without the help of a regular work paycheck.

The danger? You could run out of money before you run out of breath.

It's not just about having enough to get by for a few years. Many people fail to consider the possibility of living well into their 90s or even reaching the 100-year mark. Without proper planning, your assets may be depleted by the time you're 85, leaving you financially vulnerable in your later years.

Solution: Plan for longevity. Assume you'll live to at least 90 or 95, if not 100. This will help you adjust your savings goals, withdrawal rates, and investment strategy. Use conservative withdrawal rates (3-4% per year) to ensure you don't deplete your funds too quickly. Additionally, consider annuities or longevity insurance if you're concerned about outliving your savings.

2. Believing Healthcare Is "Covered"

In many countries, there is a sense of security that comes with universal or public healthcare systems. People often assume that healthcare will be entirely covered when they retire, but that's rarely the case. Even in countries with national health services, like the UK's NHS or Canada's healthcare system, the costs of healthcare after retirement can still be substantial.

In other places, such as the United States, private healthcare systems can lead to high out-of-pocket costs, even for those with Medicare or similar programs.

The danger? Your "comfortable" retirement could be consumed by medical bills or the high cost of long-term care.

Healthcare expenses can be unpredictable, especially in the later years of life. One unexpected illness or injury could wipe out years of savings, leaving you with little financial room to manoeuvre. This is especially true in countries that don't cover long-term care expenses, such as nursing homes or home healthcare.

Solution: Don't assume healthcare is fully covered. Research the specifics of healthcare coverage in your country, and be sure to budget for premiums, deductibles, and co-pays. In many cases, supplemental health insurance or long-term care insurance (LTC) may be advisable to mitigate these costs. If you're in a country with public health insurance, investigate additional private insurance options to cover gaps in care.

Remember: Healthcare isn't just about treating physical illnesses; it also includes essential services like vision care, dental health, and other areas of the body that can deteriorate with age. These aspects of health often require ongoing attention and can become significant costs in retirement, yet they are frequently not fully covered by public healthcare systems or insurance plans in many countries.

3. Taking Social Security Too Early

In many countries, government-sponsored social safety nets (such as Social Security, the State Pension, or similar programs) offer regular income in retirement. But, while it's tempting to start receiving these benefits as soon as possible, doing so early often means locking in a lower monthly payout for the rest of your life.

For example, in the United States, you can start claiming Social Security benefits as early as 62, but your monthly benefit will be reduced by a certain percentage for every year you claim before your full retirement age (which is 66-67, depending on the year you were born). The same concept applies in many countries with national pension systems, where early access can result in permanent reductions.

The danger? You sacrifice thousands of dollars in long-term income for short-term financial relief that you might not even need.

Taking early social security may be appropriate for some, but many people do so out of anxiety or a lack of understanding about how the system works. If you wait until your full retirement age, or even until 70, depending on the country, you could significantly increase your monthly benefit.

Solution: If you're healthy and have other income sources, delay claiming government pension benefits until your full retirement age (or even 70) to maximise your monthly payout. View these benefits as longevity insurance. The additional income in your later years could provide essential security.

4. Ignoring Inflation

Inflation is a silent threat that many retirees overlook. A dollar today won't buy you the same amount of goods and services as it will in 10, 20, or 30 years. Even with relatively low inflation rates, 2% to 3% annually, this can dramatically erode your purchasing power over time.

The danger? You may retire comfortably but find yourself struggling to afford necessities later in life.

While your income may be fixed once you retire, whether from savings, pensions, or social security, your expenses will continue to increase due to inflation. Things like groceries, utilities, and even healthcare costs may rise, and without a strategy to counteract this, you could find yourself financially strained in your later years.

Solution: Don't rely solely on "safe" investments like bonds or cash. Keep part of your portfolio invested in growth-oriented assets, such as stocks or equity-based funds. Growth assets, despite their risks, tend to outpace inflation over the long term. A well-balanced investment strategy can help protect your purchasing power.

5. Failing to Plan for Taxes

In retirement, you may find that your tax bill is higher than you expected. Depending on the country, many retirement savings vehicles, such as pensions, 401(k)s, or IRAs (Individual Retirement Accounts), are subject to taxation when you withdraw funds. In addition, social security or national pension benefits may also be taxed in some countries.

The danger? You thought you were in a lower tax bracket, but your retirement withdrawals push you into a higher one, potentially eroding your nest egg faster than you anticipated.

Taxes on retirement income can be unpredictable, especially if you're withdrawing from tax-deferred accounts like traditional IRAs or pensions. Furthermore, some countries impose taxes on social security or pension benefits, and you may also face taxes on required minimum distributions (RMDs) from your retirement accounts.

Solution: Diversify your retirement income sources. For example, Roth IRAs, Health Savings Accounts (HSAs), municipal bonds, and other tax-advantaged accounts can provide income with reduced or no taxes. It's also wise to work with a tax advisor to create a tax-smart withdrawal strategy. Proper tax planning can help you minimise your tax liability in retirement.

6. Supporting Adult Children Financially

It's natural to want to help your children, but doing so at the expense of your own retirement security can be a dangerous gamble. Many retirees fall into the trap of using their retirement funds to help their children with major life expenses, like buying a home, paying for education, or supporting grandchildren.

The danger? You may drain your nest egg to help your children and later find yourself financially dependent on them in your old age.

While it's admirable to want to support your children, it's important not to jeopardise your own financial future. Helping them today could leave you vulnerable to financial insecurity in the future. You can read more on supporting your children in the chapter "The Hidden cost of Love."

Solution: Set clear boundaries. Offer emotional support and guidance, but don't compromise your retirement by going into debt or draining your savings. As the saying goes, "You can get loans for education, but you can't get a loan for retirement." Make sure you have your financial future secured before helping others.

7. Assuming You'll "Spend Less" in Retirement

Many people assume that they will automatically spend less money in retirement. While it's true that some costs, like commuting or work-related expenses, may decrease, other costs can increase significantly in retirement. Things like travel, hobbies, medical bills, and gifts for family members can create unexpected financial burdens.

The danger? You may drastically underestimate your retirement expenses and end up overspending in the early years.

While you may not have to buy work clothes or pay for transportation to an office, new expenses may arise as you adjust to life without a job. Retirement can be a time for travel and pursuing passions, but without careful planning, these activities can quickly drain your savings.

Solution: Build a detailed retirement budget, factoring in both fixed and variable expenses. Track your spending over time and adjust for inflation. Your retirement spending needs may differ from your pre-retirement spending, so it's important to calculate and plan accordingly.

8. Not Having a Plan for "What's Next"

Retirement isn't just a financial event, it's a psychological one. Many people spend their working years dreaming of retirement, but when they finally reach it, they often struggle with what to do next. Without a clear sense of purpose, retirees can feel lost, bored, or disconnected.

The danger? Boredom, depression, and even declining health can creep in when you don't have a fulfilling plan for how to spend your time.

It's important to have a "what's next" plan that goes beyond finances.

This plan should include how you want to fill your days with meaning, purpose, and connection.

Solution: Develop a non-financial retirement plan. What will you do to stay mentally and physically active? Volunteer, travel, learn a new skill, start a hobby, or even take on part-time work if you want to stay engaged and feel productive.

9. Falling for Scams and Bad Investments

Unfortunately, retirees are often targets for financial scams and investment fraud. With retirement savings in hand and a desire for safe, guaranteed returns, many retirees fall prey to Ponzi schemes, high-pressure sales tactics, and poorly understood financial products.

The danger? You could lose a significant portion of your savings in a scam or bad investment decision.

While scams vary widely across different regions, one thing is clear: fraudulent schemes often promise high returns with little risk. Unfortunately, these promises are rarely as good as they seem.

Solution: Always be cautious and sceptical of any "too-good-to-be-true" offers. Only invest in things you fully understand and always check the credentials of anyone offering financial advice. If something sounds too good to be true, it usually is. Work with a certified financial advisor who is legally bound to act in your best interest.

10. Neglecting Estate and Legacy Planning

Thinking about death isn't easy, but neglecting to plan for your estate could cause unnecessary stress for your loved ones. Without a will, a living trust, or healthcare directives, your estate may end up in legal limbo, potentially resulting in high legal fees, family disputes, and large tax burdens.

The danger? Your legacy could be lost or contested, causing financial and emotional strain for your heirs.

Estate planning isn't just for the ultra-wealthy, it's something everyone should do to ensure that your wishes are honoured, and your loved ones are taken care of.

Solution: Create a will, update your beneficiaries, assign power of attorney, and consider a living trust. Estate planning can provide peace of mind for you and your family, ensuring your legacy is passed on according to your wishes.

Our Story – Our Financial Worries

When I retired, we thought we had it all planned, holidays, dining out, and a steady income stream. But what we didn't expect was how hard it would be to access some of our own money.

The government systems, it turns out, aren't always retirement friendly. In our case, we were denied an expected payment because we had "earned too much" in 2023, despite it being 2025. We spent six stressful months trying to resolve it. The delay hit us hard until they finally released the funds.

Retirement comes with surprises, and not all of them are pleasant. But these challenges are part of the process. If you face them with patience, determination, and a bit of humour, they won't stop you from enjoying the freedom you've earned.

Retirement Is a Journey

Avoiding these hidden dangers doesn't require genius, it requires awareness, discipline, and proactive planning. You don't have to fear retirement, but you do need to be prepared.

Underestimating Your Lifespan

"Planning for retirement without planning for longevity is like setting sail without checking your fuel. You might enjoy the early breeze, until you're stranded far from shore."

One of the most overlooked, yet most impactful, risks in retirement planning is longevity risk, the very real possibility that you may live significantly longer than you expect. While this might sound like good news (and it is!), living a long life comes with serious financial implications.

Today, thanks to global advancements in healthcare, sanitation, nutrition, and chronic disease management, people across the world are living longer than ever before. Yet when it comes to retirement planning, most individuals still underestimate how long they'll live, or worse, avoid thinking about it altogether.

This chapter dives into why longevity risk matters, how it can quietly unravel even the most meticulous retirement plan, and what you can do to safeguard your financial future against this increasingly common outcome.

1. The Global Shift: We're Living Longer

Over the last few decades, life expectancy has increased dramatically around the world. According to the World Health Organisation (WHO), the global average life expectancy in 2024 is over 73 years, with many developed countries boasting averages in the late 70s and early 80s. However, averages are just that, averages. They hide the fact that many people now live into their 90s or even beyond 100.

For example:

- In **Japan**, average life expectancy exceeds 84 years, with a large and growing population of centenarians.
- In **the European Union**, the average is around 81 years, with women typically living longer than men.
- In **the United States**, it's about 77–79 years, though this varies by ethnicity and geography.
- In **Australia, Canada, and Scandinavia**, life expectancies also hover between 80 and 84 years.

Crucially, if you've made it to 60 or 65 in good health, your odds of reaching 90 or 95 increase significantly. Yet most retirement planning ends at 85, often even earlier. That disconnect can create a devastating shortfall in your retirement funding.

2. Why Underestimating Longevity is Dangerous

When you plan for a 20-year retirement but live 30 or 35 years, you risk outliving your savings. This is known in financial planning as "longevity risk," and it's often referred to as the "mother of all risks" in retirement, because it amplifies every other financial risk.

You Risk Running Out of Money

If you retire at 60 and plan for 20 years of income, but live to 95, those last 15 years could be financially devastating. You might rely entirely on government pensions or be forced to reduce your lifestyle drastically.

Inflation Eats Away at Purchasing Power

The longer you live, the more inflation erodes your spending power. Even at a modest inflation rate of 2% per year, your costs could double over 35 years.

Healthcare Costs Compound

Age-related health issues become more frequent and expensive as you age. Long-term care needs, such as assisted living or in-home care, can quickly drain whatever funds remain late in retirement.

You Lose Flexibility

Without sufficient savings, retirees may be forced to sell assets, downsize homes, or rely on family for support. These aren't always practical or desired solutions, particularly in your later years when health and mobility may be declining.

3. Psychological Bias: Why We Underestimate Lifespan

Despite the clear trends, many people still fail to plan for a long life. Why?

- **Optimism Bias:** People tend to believe that negative outcomes are more likely to happen to others, not themselves.

- **Present Bias:** We prioritise today's needs over long-term planning, especially when retirement feels far off.
- **Mortality Salience:** Simply put, many people don't like thinking about aging or death, so they avoid the subject entirely.
- **Family History Myopia:** People base their life expectancy on parents or grandparents, forgetting that medical advances and healthier lifestyles can significantly increase longevity from one generation to the next.

4. Planning as if You'll Live to 100

A simple mindset shift, plan to 100, can be one of the most effective ways to bulletproof your retirement plan. It may feel extreme, but in most developed nations, living to 90 or 95 is no longer an outlier. Planning to 100 provides a cushion that helps you avoid the pitfalls of longevity risk.

Use Conservative Withdrawal Rates

The "4% rule" is a classic benchmark in retirement planning: withdraw 4% of your portfolio annually to make it last about 30 years. But for longer retirements, some advisors recommend 3–3.5% instead.

Example:

- $1 million at 4% = $40,000/year
- $1 million at 3% = $30,000/year (more conservative, longer-lasting)

Use Retirement Calculators with Long Time Horizons

Make sure any online or advisor-based planning tools you use are set to a 95–100-year horizon, not just 85.

You may need to manually adjust assumptions or override default life expectancy settings.

Account for Inflation Over 30–40 Years

If you're planning a long retirement, inflation must be factored in across multiple decades. This means keeping part of your portfolio in assets that grow over time (like stocks) rather than entirely in low-yield, "safe" investments.

5. Tools to Mitigate Longevity Risk

Thankfully, several financial tools and strategies can help manage longevity risk, regardless of where you live. These include:

5.1. Life Annuities

Annuities provide guaranteed income for life. Once relatively unpopular, they are regaining attention as a tool for longevity protection. Different countries offer various forms, like lifetime annuities in the UK or Australia's retirement income streams.

While annuities may not offer high returns, they provide peace of mind by ensuring you won't run out of income no matter how long you live.

5.2. Longevity Insurance (Deferred Annuities)

This product provides income starting at a later age (say, 85), acting as a financial backstop for extreme longevity. This allows you to spend more freely in your 60s and 70s, knowing support will kick in later if needed.

5.3. Government Pension Delays

In countries like the U.S., UK, and Canada, deferring your government pension can increase your monthly benefit significantly. For example:

- **U.S. Social Security:** Delaying past full retirement age (up to 70) can increase payouts by 8% per year.
- **UK State Pension:** Delaying increases your weekly pension by around 1% for every 9 weeks you defer. This effectively gives you a higher, inflation-adjusted "paycheck" for life, helping offset longevity risk.

5.4. Diversified Portfolio with Growth Assets

A mix of income-generating and growth-oriented investments can help your savings outpace inflation over the long term. Equities are generally considered riskier, but over decades, they have historically provided superior returns that support longer lifespans.

6. Realistic Budgeting for a Long Retirement

Many retirees front-load their retirement spending, using a large chunk of their savings in the early years. While travel and leisure in your 60s and 70s are important, it's critical not to ignore the spending demands of your 80s and 90s.

Plan your budget in phases:

- **Phase 1 (60s–early 70s):** Active years, higher discretionary spending (travel, hobbies).
- **Phase 2 (late 70s–80s):** Slower lifestyle, rising healthcare costs.

- **Phase 3 (late 80s–100+):** Potential need for assisted living, in-home care, and medical assistance.

Your financial plan should evolve with these stages in mind. Leaving enough reserve for the final phase is crucial in protecting yourself from longevity-related financial stress.

7. Case Study: The Cost of Underestimating Longevity

Claire and Robert: a couple from Melbourne, Australia. They retired at 62 with $800,000 in superannuation savings. They planned for a 25-year retirement, expecting their money to last until age 87.

By age 83, they had already spent 85% of their funds due to medical costs, inflation, and helping family members financially. Robert passed away at 84, but Claire, still healthy, found herself dependent almost entirely on the Old Age Pension.

Had they planned for a longer retirement and set aside funds for longevity, Claire could have maintained a better standard of living well into her 90s.

8. Family Implications of Outliving Savings

Longevity doesn't just affect you; it impacts your family. Running out of money in your 90s may mean:

- Becoming financially dependent upon adult children.
- Having to sell property or downsize in ways that affect inheritance planning.

- Being unable to afford quality long-term care.

Longevity planning, therefore, isn't just about numbers, it's about preserving your dignity, independence, and legacy.

9. What You Can Do Today

To safeguard your future, consider taking these practical steps now:

✅ Review your retirement planning tools and make sure they account for a lifespan up to age 100.
✅ Work with a financial planner to stress-test your income against different longevity scenarios.
✅ Explore annuities or longevity insurance products available in your country.
✅ Delay government pensions if possible to secure higher long-term income.
✅ Review your investment allocation and consider including long-term growth assets.
✅ Recalculate your withdrawal strategy using a 30–35 year retirement horizon.

10. Final Thoughts: Plan to Live, Not Just to Retire

Too often, retirement is viewed as an endpoint. But it's the beginning of a long, dynamic chapter of life. Underestimating how long this chapter lasts can mean cutting it short, not in years, but in quality and freedom.

Plan not just for the retirement you expect, but for the one you don't see coming. Embrace the possibility of longevity, and let your plan reflect not only financial prudence, but hope, health, and resilience.

The Healthcare Illusion

"The biggest myth about retirement healthcare is that it will be taken care of. The truth? You're likely more exposed than you think, and it could be your most expensive oversight."

When planning for retirement, many people put healthcare in the category of "already handled." Whether it's a national health system, a government-sponsored medical plan, or insurance through a former employer, there's often a dangerous assumption: that medical expenses will be minimal or fully covered.

Healthcare in retirement is rarely free, and it's almost never complete. It's a complex, multi-layered issue that affects retirees around the world, regardless of where you live. From out-of-pocket costs to uncovered services like dental, vision, and long-term care, the belief that you won't have to worry about healthcare is one of the costliest retirement myths out there.

In this chapter, we'll break down why healthcare in retirement is more expensive than most anticipate, what costs are commonly overlooked, and how to proactively build healthcare planning into your long-term financial strategy.

1. Why the "Covered" Myth Persists

In countries with universal healthcare, such as the UK, Canada, much of Europe, Australia, and New Zealand, there's a pervasive belief that once you retire, your healthcare needs will be met by the government. Meanwhile, in countries like the U.S., where Medicare or equivalent systems kick in around age 65, retirees often assume that enrolling means the end of medical expenses.

Here's the truth: no system covers everything. Not even close.

Most healthcare systems provide baseline coverage for essential medical services, but they often exclude or partially cover a wide range of costs, including:

- Prescription drugs
- Dental and vision care
- Hearing aids
- Physical therapy
- Mental health services
- In-home nursing
- Long-term residential care
- Private hospital treatment or faster access to specialists

Even routine medical care can come with co-pays, deductibles, or service caps. In fact, a large portion of healthcare costs in retirement is not covered by public plans at all, especially as people age and require more complex or prolonged care.

2. The True Cost of Healthcare in Retirement

Let's look at the numbers:

- In the United States, a healthy retired couple can expect to spend between $300,000 and $400,000 USD on healthcare throughout retirement, even with Medicare. This includes premiums, out-of-pocket expenses, and long-term care.

- In Canada, while basic care is covered, retirees still pay for prescription drugs, dental work, and long-term care. Out-of-pocket expenses can reach $6,000–$10,000 CAD per year.

- In the UK, while the NHS offers robust coverage, waiting times and exclusions push many retirees to buy private insurance, especially for dental, vision, and elective procedures.

- In Australia, the public system (Medicare) requires co-payments for specialists and does not cover many out-of-hospital services. Most retirees purchase private health insurance, with costs climbing significantly with age.

- In Europe, costs vary widely between countries, but private insurance is often required to fill coverage gaps, and out-of-pocket spending is rising due to aging populations and strained public systems.

The pattern is global: retirees consistently underestimate their healthcare needs and overestimate what's covered.

3. What's Commonly Left Out

Healthcare in retirement is about much more than hospital visits and routine check-ups. The real budget-breakers often lie in what the system doesn't cover.

a. Dental Care

As people age, dental health becomes more complicated and expensive. Implants, dentures, root canals, and gum disease treatments are common, and almost universally excluded from public healthcare coverage.

b. Vision and Eye Health

Glasses, cataract surgeries, eye exams, and conditions like glaucoma may be partially covered, but most vision-related costs require private payment or supplemental insurance.

c. Hearing Loss

Hearing aids and hearing services are expensive and often fall outside standard coverage. Yet age-related hearing loss affects over 30% of people over 65 worldwide.

d. Prescription Medications

Drug plans vary enormously. In some countries, essential medications are subsidised, but brand-name or newer therapies can be prohibitively expensive. In others, retirees pay the full cost of prescriptions out-of-pocket.

e. Mental Health Support

Conditions such as depression, anxiety, and cognitive decline (including dementia) are common in later life but underfunded in most systems. Access to therapy, support groups, and psychiatric care may be limited or costly.

f. Mobility and Rehabilitation Equipment

Wheelchairs, walkers, home adjustments, and rehabilitation services are often under-covered or capped at low reimbursement levels.

g. Long-Term Care

The biggest gap is often long-term care. Nursing homes assisted living facilities, and in-home caregivers typically are not covered by standard medical plans or are only partially subsidised based on strict eligibility.

4. The Compounding Risk of Age

Aging is expensive. While you may enter retirement in good health, statistically speaking, the likelihood of needing medical support increases significantly with age:

- By age 70, many begin facing chronic conditions like diabetes, arthritis, or cardiovascular issues.
- By age 80, the need for help with daily tasks, like dressing, cooking, or bathing, rises sharply.
- Dementia and cognitive decline affect approximately 1 in 6 people over 80, creating a need for 24/7 supervision.

The later years of retirement (the 80s and 90s) are where healthcare costs often spike dramatically. Without preparation, these costs can devastate a retirement portfolio or force difficult decisions, such as downsizing, selling assets, or relying on family for financial support.

5. Missteps That Exacerbate the Problem

Beyond assuming healthcare is covered, retirees make several common mistakes that worsen the situation:

- **Failing to Buy Supplemental Insurance:** In many countries, supplemental or private health insurance fills crucial gaps. Failing to secure this early can lead to denial or much higher costs later due to pre-existing conditions.
- **Not Budgeting for Out-of-Pocket Costs:** Many retirees don't include healthcare as a distinct line in their retirement budget, leading to underfunding and unexpected withdrawals.
- **Delaying Care Due to Cost Concerns:** Postponing treatment or screenings can lead to worse health outcomes, and higher costs down the road.
- **Ignoring Preventive Health:** Staying healthy reduces costs. Skipping regular exercise, social engagement, or diet management can accelerate chronic conditions.

6. How to Proactively Plan for Healthcare in Retirement

There are no guarantees, but you can take smart steps to prepare for healthcare's financial impact.

a. Create a Dedicated Healthcare Budget

Include a specific line item in your retirement plan for medical expenses, broken down by premiums, deductibles, medications, dental, vision, and expected out-of-pocket care. Use country-specific data or a financial planner to get accurate estimates.

b. Purchase Supplemental Insurance

Research your options:

- **Private health insurance** to cover services excluded from public systems.
- **Dental and vision plans** tailored for retirees.
- **Critical illness coverage** or **hospital cash insurance** that pays lump sums during serious illness or hospitalisation.

  These options vary widely by country and provider but can be invaluable for protecting retirement assets.

c. Consider Long-Term Care Insurance

Long-term care coverage, where available, is a critical component of retirement planning. These policies help pay for assisted living, home health aides, or nursing care that public systems typically don't cover.

Some people opt for hybrid life insurance policies with long-term care riders. Others set aside specific savings earmarked for long-term care. In countries where private insurance isn't available, self-funding strategies are essential.

d. Delay Retirement or Phase Out Gradually

Working a few extra years often means staying on employer health plans longer and deferring government coverage (which may come with increased benefits if delayed). It also provides more time to save specifically for healthcare needs.

e. Stay Healthy

Investing in your health now is the most cost-effective strategy. Eat well, exercise regularly, manage stress, and stay socially active. Preventive care and lifestyle choices can significantly reduce long-term healthcare costs.

Case Studies

Anita and George are two retirees in their early 60s. Both live in Germany and have access to a strong public healthcare system.

- **Anita** assumes everything will be covered. She doesn't buy supplemental insurance, skips budgeting for dental and long-term care, and spends heavily in her early retirement.
- **George**, meanwhile, works with a planner to identify gaps in coverage. He buys supplemental insurance, sets aside funds for future care, and maintains a healthy lifestyle.

By age 80, Anita needs a hip replacement and extended rehabilitation. She's surprised to find her public plan doesn't cover private rehab or mobility equipment, and she struggles financially. George undergoes the same surgery but uses his insurance and savings to cover everything comfortably.

Our Story – Our Health

When the news of my redundancy arrived, it hit hard, not just financially, but emotionally. My wife and I had already started discussing retirement, but this sudden change forced us to confront our future more urgently.

Among the first decisions we made was to check on our health.

We scheduled appointments with our doctor to get a full picture of where we stood. It was a sensible move, but one I'd recommend to anyone nearing retirement, regardless of circumstances. That visit proved to be more eye-opening than I expected.

The doctor ran a suite of tests and then looked at me with that calm seriousness you come to recognise over time. I was flagged as a pre-diabetic. It wasn't a crisis, but it was a clear sign that I needed to make changes. My wife, thankfully, breezed through her check-up with flying colours. But for me, it was a sobering reminder that time catches up to all of us in different ways.

We're fortunate to live in Canada, where diabetes care is covered under our public healthcare system. Because of this, I didn't have to worry about huge medical bills, just a manageable out-of-pocket cost for prescriptions. Even so, those small expenses added up, and it reminded me how essential it is to include health contingencies in any retirement budget.

Looking back, I'm grateful we took that step when we did. It gave us a clearer view of what we were walking into and allowed us to adjust before problems grew larger. Today, I manage my health carefully, and we've both embraced a more mindful lifestyle. It's not a burden, it's an investment in being able to enjoy this new chapter for as long as possible.

So, since you are thinking about retirement, here's my advice: put your health on the checklist. Make time for a full check-up. Understand what your body is telling you. And make sure your finances include room for the "what-ifs." Because when it comes to retirement, being proactive about your health isn't just smart, it's essential.

7. Don't Rely on Hope. Rely on a Plan

Hope is not a strategy. Governments are under increasing strain as aging populations grow, and healthcare costs rise. Future benefits may be trimmed, means-tested, or delayed. It's essential to plan as if you will bear most of the cost and consider any public support a bonus.

Key steps to remember:

- ✅ Research your country's healthcare coverage and identify what's excluded.
- ✅ Budget for medical expenses over a 30+ year retirement horizon.
- ✅ Purchase appropriate insurance while you're still healthy enough to qualify.
- ✅ Explore long-term care planning early.
- ✅ Take care of your health, because prevention is the best form of savings.

Final Thoughts On life Expectancy

Retirement is meant to be enjoyed, not feared. But the joy of those years depends heavily on your health, and your ability to manage the costs that come with it.

Don't let the illusion of "covered" care lull you into a false sense of security. Whether you live in a country with universal healthcare or one that relies more on private systems, the gaps are real, and the costs are rising.

Build healthcare planning into your retirement strategy from the start. Your future self, healthier, safer, and more financially secure, will thank you for it.

Early vs. Delayed Government Pensions

One of the earliest, and most impactful, decisions you'll face as you approach retirement is whether to start drawing your pension early or to delay it. It seems straightforward at first: take the money now or wait and get more later. But like many aspects of retirement, the answer is layered with personal circumstance, financial strategy, and risk tolerance.

Let's begin with the appeal of taking your pension early. For many, the thought of accessing those funds as soon as they become available (often at age 60 or 62, depending on your scheme) is attractive. The benefits are clear: more financial flexibility, earlier freedom from work, and the chance to enjoy your healthier, more active years with the resources to do so. If your health is uncertain, or if you've been in a physically demanding job and simply can't continue working, early retirement can be not just practical, but necessary.

However, there are trade-offs. Taking your pension early usually means accepting a reduced monthly payment for life. Pension providers apply an "actuarial reduction" to account for the longer time they'll be paying you. This reduction can be steep, sometimes 20% to 30% less than what you'd receive by waiting until full retirement age, or even longer. Over a 20 or 30-year retirement, those lower monthly payments can add up to a significant difference.

On the other hand, delaying your pension, even just a few years, can substantially increase your monthly income. Many pension schemes offer incentives for deferring, often adding between 6% and 8% to your payout per year of delay. If you're still in good health and have other income sources to bridge the gap, this strategy can lead to a much stronger financial foundation in your later years. It's also a form of longevity insurance: if you live into your 80s or 90s, that higher income can make a meaningful difference.

But waiting comes with its own risks. You're forgoing income now in the hope of a longer, more secure future. If something unexpected happens, health issues, market downturns, or changing family needs, you might find yourself wishing you'd taken the money earlier. It's also worth remembering that not all of retirement is created equal: your 60s and early 70s are typically your most active years. Having the financial freedom to enjoy those years can be worth the smaller cheque.

Ultimately, this decision comes down to a combination of math, health, and lifestyle goals. There is no one-size-fits-all answer. What matters is being informed, understanding the terms of your pension scheme, knowing your expected expenses, and being realistic about your future.

Let's compare how four major countries handle the timing of public retirement benefits. While each system differs in structure, they all share a common feature: you receive more if you wait.

Canada – Canada Pension Plan (CPP) & Old Age Security (OAS)

- **Standard Age:** 65
- **Earliest Claim:** 60 (CPP), 65 (OAS)
- **Incentives to Delay:**
    - **CPP:** For each month you delay past 65, your benefit increases by 0.7% (up to 42% more by age 70).

  - **Early Claiming Penalty:** Reduces by 0.6% per month before 65 (up to 36% less at age 60).

Delaying CPP to age 70 can result in 42% higher monthly income.

United Kingdom – State Pension

- **Standard Age:** Currently 66 (rising to 67+ in future)
- **No Early Claiming**: You cannot claim early.
- **Incentives to Delay:**
  - If you delay by at least 9 weeks, your pension increases by 1% for every 9 weeks delayed (~5.8% more per year).

Delaying one year can increase income by nearly 6% annually.

Australia – Age Pension

- **Standard Age:** 67 (based on birth year)
- **Means-Tested:** Based on income and assets.
- **Early Claiming:** Not permitted.
- **Delaying Strategy:**
  - Pension Bonus Scheme (now closed) was used to encourage delayed retirement. Current options focus on personal savings, superannuation, or working longer.

Although early claiming isn't allowed, delaying retirement often increases superannuation savings and tax benefits.

United States – Social Security ***(for comparison)***

- **Full Retirement Age (FRA):** 66–67 (based on birth year)
- **Earliest Claim:** 62
- **Delay Bonus:** Increases 8% per year if delayed up to age 70
- **Early Penalty:** Reduced by up to 30% if claimed at 62

Delaying from 62 to 70 increases monthly payments by up to **76%.**

The Takeaway

Regardless of where you live:

- **Waiting** = More income for life
- **Early** = Less income, permanently

Understanding your country's specific rules empowers you to make decisions that maximise long-term security, not just short-term relief.

Failing to Plan for Taxes

Many people assume retirement equals lower taxes. After all, you're no longer earning a full salary, so surely your tax bill goes down, right?

Wrong.

Failing to plan for taxes in retirement is one of the most common, and costly, mistakes retirees make. Around the world, retirees often find themselves paying more taxes than they expected, losing a big chunk of their carefully saved nest egg.

Whether you live in Australia, South Africa, the UK, Canada, Germany, India, or Singapore, retirement taxation is complex, and each system has its own traps. Without a plan, taxes can quietly drain your income year after year.

Retirement Income Is Still Taxable

Across countries, retirement income is taxed in different ways depending on its source:

Income Type	Is It Taxed in Retirement?
Government pension	Often partially or fully taxable
Private/employer pension	Usually, taxable
Rental income	Taxable in almost every country

Investment income	Taxable based on local laws
Withdrawals from savings	Varies, some are tax-free, others are not

For example:

- In the United States, Social Security is taxable above certain income levels, and withdrawals from traditional retirement accounts (like IRAs) are fully taxed as income.
- In Canada, withdrawals from RRSPs are taxable, but TFSA income is not.
- In India, pension income is taxable unless specifically exempt, and senior citizens still file returns.
- In the UK, income from private pensions and annuities is taxed after a personal allowance.
- In Germany, pensions are partially taxed depending on retirement year and other income.
- In Australia, superannuation withdrawals may be tax-free or taxed depending on age and structure.

No matter where you live, assuming your retirement income is tax-free is a mistake.

How Taxes Can Eat Your Nest Egg

Let's take an example:

- You saved $500,000 for retirement.
- You withdraw $30,000 per year.
- In a 20% tax bracket, you're paying $6,000 in taxes annually.

Over 25 years, that's $150,000 lost, money you might not have accounted for.

Now multiply this by the additional taxes on investments, pensions, and other income, and the real tax burden becomes even heavier.

The Tax Traps Retirees Fall Into

1. **Not Diversifying Income Sources**
   Relying solely on taxable accounts or pensions means more predictable, and higher, taxes.
2. **Forgetting Required Withdrawals**
   Some countries force you to begin withdrawing from retirement accounts (like RMDs in the U.S. or RRIFs in Canada), which pushes you into higher tax brackets.
3. **Selling Investments Without Planning**
   Selling real estate, shares, or business assets without understanding capital gains taxes can cause massive, unexpected tax bills.
4. **Collecting Multiple Pensions**
   In many systems, collecting multiple pensions (state + private) can phase out benefits or push you into higher tax brackets.
5. **Not Considering Cross-Border Tax Rules**
   If you retire abroad or hold foreign investments, you could face double taxation or need complex tax treaty planning.

Tax-Efficient Retirement Planning Strategies

Here are globally applicable tips that can help retirees in any country:

1. Diversify Tax Exposure

Plan for three types of income:

- **Taxable**: Pensions, rentals, interest
- **Tax-deferred**: Traditional retirement accounts (RRSPs, IRAs, etc.)
- **Tax-free**: TFSAs, Roth IRAs, ISAs, or municipal bond income

Having income from all three lets you control your tax rate in retirement.

2. Use Tax-Advantaged Accounts

Every country has some form of tax-advantaged savings vehicle:

- **Canada**: TFSA, RRSP
- **UK**: ISA, Pension Plans
- **Australia**: Superannuation
- **India**: PPF, NPS
- **Germany**: Riester and Rürup pensions
- **U.S.**: Roth IRA, HSA

Use them strategically for long-term gain.

3. Plan Withdrawals Wisely

Don't blindly start drawing from accounts. Work with an advisor (or use calculators) to:

- Withdraw from the most tax-efficient sources first
- Spread out large gains over multiple tax years
- Avoid higher tax brackets and benefit phase-outs

4. Understand Your Country's Rules

Take time to understand:

- Tax treatment of pensions
- Local and national income thresholds

- Whether you qualify for senior tax credits or rebates

These small details can save you thousands annually.

5. If You Move Abroad, Know the Tax Treaty

Many retirees move to lower-cost countries. If you do:

- Research tax treaties between your home and destination country
- Avoid double taxation
- Know what income is taxed where

For example

- U.S. citizens must file taxes even when living abroad
- The UK taxes based on residency
- Canada ends taxation for non-residents, but some pensions remain taxable
- India has limited pension tax relief for non-residents

Final Thought

It's tempting to think taxes go away when your paychecks stop. But retirement is often more tax-sensitive than working life.

If you fail to plan, governments may take more than their fair share of your savings.

A tax-efficient plan can add years to your financial independence.

The Hidden Cost of Love

For many parents around the world, love for their children endures for a lifetime. Even after children become adults, the desire to offer help and protection remains strong. But in retirement, a time when income often becomes fixed and personal resources finite, offering financial support to adult children can quietly become one of the most significant threats to long-term security.

While the instinct to help is natural and often noble, it's crucial to balance generosity with practicality. Across countries and cultures, more and more retirees find themselves dipping into their own limited resources to help their grown children. The question isn't whether this support is loving, it's whether it is sustainable.

A Global Trend: Parents as Financial Safety Nets

Across continents, cultures, and economic systems, one pattern has emerged: adult children are increasingly relying on their parents for financial assistance. Whether due to rising housing costs, stagnant wages, economic downturns, or global crises, more young adults are turning to their parents not just for emotional support, but for money.

In many parts of the world, multigenerational households have become common, not only due to tradition, but also because of financial necessity. In wealthier countries, parents may contribute toward university fees, help with first-time home purchases, or cover day-to-day expenses. In developing countries, parental support can stretch to include everything from paying for weddings to subsidising basic living costs for unemployed children.

Whatever the motivation or circumstance, the financial impact on retirees can be severe, especially when this support becomes habitual.

1. Shrinking the Retirement Fund

The most obvious danger is the depletion of retirement savings. Unlike during working years, retirees generally don't have the opportunity to earn more income through full-time employment. Once savings are spent, there's little to no way to replenish them.

Even seemingly small contributions, covering a rent payment here, helping with school fees there, can snowball over time. Many retirees underestimate the cumulative effect of years of financial support. Add inflation and market volatility to the equation, and the real value of your savings can erode faster than anticipated.

Retirement is supposed to provide stability, but draining your nest egg for others may compromise your own comfort and security.

2. Delaying or Sacrificing Retirement Goals

People around the world retire with dreams, travel, community involvement, leisure, time with grandchildren, or simply the ability to rest. But if you're continually diverting resources to support your adult children, your own dreams may suffer.

Some retirees end up postponing travel, living more frugally than necessary, or even re-entering the workforce to make ends meet. Others may forgo important medical procedures, delay home maintenance, or sell assets just to maintain balance.

Supporting your children at the cost of your own plans can lead not only to financial stress but emotional resentment.

3. Creating Dependency

Helping adult children in times of need is natural. But when that help becomes regular or expected, it can prevent them from achieving true independence.

Over time, this dynamic can lead to:

- Poor budgeting and financial planning on their part
- Delayed career progression or risk-taking
- Lack of motivation to solve their own financial challenges

This problem can be seen in both high-income and low-income settings. Whether you're providing cash, paying bills, or offering free housing, the unintended consequence may be enabling financial dependence rather than fostering resilience.

Dependence, once established, is hard to reverse, and this can lead to a cycle where adult children never fully mature into financially self-sufficient individuals.

4. Legal and Financial Complexity

In some countries, there are legal implications for large financial transfers, including tax reporting or inheritance issues. Even in regions where tax laws are more lenient, giving substantial or ongoing support to adult children can complicate estate planning or retirement budgeting.

In cultures where parents co-sign for loans or include their children on property deeds, there's a risk of shared liability. If the adult child defaults or mismanages resources, the parent may end up absorbing the financial fallout, at a stage in life when financial setbacks are harder to recover from.

5. Family Tension and Inequality

A common source of family conflict arises when one child receives more support than others. Even if the help is offered for legitimate reasons, a job loss, a health issue, or an unexpected crisis, siblings may perceive it as favouritism.

Such disparities can lead to:

- Sibling rivalry or jealousy
- Marital disagreements if spouses don’t agree on financial decisions
- Confusion or disputes during inheritance or estate planning

In cultures with strong traditions around family obligation and elder care, this tension can be even more pronounced, especially when resources are limited.

6. No Second Chances: Limited Recovery Time

A key difference between younger and older adults is time. When a younger person makes a financial mistake, there is time to recover. They can retrain, re-enter the workforce, or rebuild savings over several decades.

For retirees, however, the window for financial recovery is much smaller. Illness, reduced energy, or age discrimination in hiring can limit options. If you exhaust your savings or accumulate debt supporting your children, there may be no viable way to recover your financial footing.

This stark reality makes every financial decision in retirement more consequential.

Saying "No" with Compassion

Across cultures, family bonds run deep. Parents often feel guilt or fear when they consider turning down a child's request for help. In some societies, it is considered shameful not to support your children, no matter their age.

But helping your children should not mean sacrificing your own stability. Just as you once supported them when they were young, now your role is to guide them toward independence. Saying "no" doesn't mean you don't care, it means you are making a wise, long-term decision for everyone's well-being.

Setting boundaries is an act of love, not rejection.

Practical Ways to Help Without Harming

If you do choose to support your adult children, here are practical strategies to do so without endangering your retirement:

1. Set Clear Limits

Define how much you can afford to help, financially, emotionally, and in terms of time. Communicate these limits openly.

2. Offer Temporary, Not Permanent, Support

Frame assistance as short-term. Set goals and timelines. For example, agree to help with rent for six months while your child looks for work.

3. Create a Written Agreement

Even within families, a written understanding can help manage expectations and prevent misunderstandings, especially when large sums are involved.

4. Prioritise Non-Financial Support

You can offer help in many ways that don't involve money:

- Sharing accommodation for a fixed time
- Helping with job applications or networking
- Providing childcare to help them save on costs

5. Promote Financial Literacy

Encourage your children to learn about budgeting, saving, and investing. Direct them to community workshops, books, or financial advisors if possible.

Protecting Your Legacy

Supporting your adult children during difficult times is admirable. But your greatest gift may be showing them how to prepare for their own future. A well-planned, self-sufficient retirement allows you to serve as a model of financial responsibility and ensures you do not become a burden later.

Here's what a strong legacy includes:

- Teaching resilience and adaptability
- Modelling wise financial behaviour
- Leaving behind assets, not debts
- Maintaining dignity and independence

What you demonstrate in retirement, your boundaries, your decisions, your priorities, will influence how your children approach their own lives, and eventually, their own retirement.

Final Reflection

Supporting adult children in retirement is an act of love, but love must be grounded in foresight and self-respect. Around the world, the emotional pull of helping family is powerful. But so is the importance of preserving your own well-being, dignity, and peace of mind.

There is no shame in helping when you can, but there is wisdom in knowing your limits. Retirement is not just a time of rest; it's a time of stewardship. You are the caretaker of your financial health, your freedom, and your future.

Give wisely. Love fully. And remember: a strong foundation for you makes you better able to support those you love, in the ways that matter most.

The Frugal Myth

A common assumption in retirement planning is the belief that expenses will decrease once you stop working. After all, commuting costs disappear, work attire is no longer needed, and lunches at the office become a thing of the past. For many, it seems logical to assume that a simpler, quieter lifestyle will naturally cost less.

But this belief, however intuitive, is often misguided. In truth, many retirees spend as much or more in retirement, particularly during the early and later stages. Relying on the idea that "you'll need less" can lead to shortfalls, stress, and difficult choices down the road.

In this chapter, we will unpack why assuming lower spending in retirement is risky, how different phases of retirement affect expenses, and how to plan more realistically for the lifestyle you want and the life you'll live.

The Appeal of the "Spend Less" Assumption

The notion that expenses drop significantly in retirement is not baseless. There are valid reasons to expect some costs to go down:

- **Work-related expenses** disappear (e.g., commuting, uniforms, eating out).
- **Mortgage payments** may be completed if you've paid off your home.
- **Savings contribution** (to pensions, retirement plans, etc.) may end.

- **Children** may be financially independent.

For planners and advisors, this idea has traditionally formed the basis for the "replacement rate" concept, recommending that retirees plan to live on 70%–80% of their pre-retirement income.

But as retirement becomes longer, more active, and more complex, these old assumptions may no longer hold true.

The Problem: Expenses - Stay the Same, or Increase

Retirees across many countries report being surprised at how much money they continue to spend. Here's why:

1. More Free Time Means More Spending Opportunities

One of the biggest changes in retirement is having more time. That's good for your lifestyle, but it often leads to increased discretionary spending.

- **Travel and leisure**: With no job tying you down, it's natural to travel more, especially in the early years of retirement.
- **Dining out**: Meals with friends, coffee outings, and spontaneous lunches become frequent.
- **Hobbies and entertainment**: From golf and gardening to classes and crafts, hobbies cost money, and now you have time to enjoy them.

More time doesn't just mean more rest, it can mean more spending.

2. Healthcare Costs Rise with Age

Healthcare is one of the largest, and most unpredictable, expenses in retirement. As you age, the likelihood of needing medical attention, medication, and even long-term care increases.

In countries with public healthcare systems, some costs may be subsidised, but not everything is covered. In countries without universal healthcare, costs can be catastrophic without proper insurance or savings.

Common expenses include:

- Prescription drugs
- Medical devices or therapies
- Dental, vision, and hearing care
- Home modifications (e.g., ramps, safety installations)
- Private insurance or out-of-pocket services

3. Housing Costs Don't Always Disappear

Even if you've paid off your mortgage, housing often remains a significant expense.

- **Maintenance and repairs** increase as your home ages.
- **Utilities** will continue and may even rise with more time spent at home.
- **Property taxes, insurance, and fees** don't go away.
- **Downsizing** may come with unexpected costs like relocation, legal fees, or renovations.

Renters face even more unpredictability, as rental prices tend to rise over time in most countries.

4. Family Obligations Continue

Many retirees find themselves financially supporting family members well into retirement:

- Helping adult children or grandchildren
- Caring for elderly parents
- Paying for weddings, education, or emergencies

This support can strain a budget that was built under the assumption that only two people, or one, would need to be provided for.

5. Inflation and Currency Risk

The cost of goods and services tends to rise over time. While inflation rates vary by country, even low annual inflation can significantly reduce your purchasing power over a retirement lasting 20–30 years.

For retirees who live abroad or rely on foreign currencies, currency fluctuations can impact affordability, especially for expats or those drawing pensions in one country and living in another.

6. Lifestyle Expectations Don't Shrink Overnight

Many retirees are not content to live a drastically “simpler” life. If you’re used to a certain standard, dining out, driving a good car, traveling occasionally, it’s difficult to scale back without feeling deprived.

Retirement is not the time most people want to compromise. In fact, many view it as a reward. If your plan assumes that you’ll “just need less,” you may end up disappointed or underfunded.

The Retirement Spending Curve

Retirement is not a single, static phase. It unfolds in stages, and spending typically varies across these stages:

1. Active Retirement (Ages ~60–75)

This phase is often called the "go-go years."

- Retirees are healthy, active, and eager to explore.
- Travel, hobbies, and social events are frequent.
- Spending is often higher than during working years.

2. Slower Retirement (Ages ~75–85)

Sometimes called the "slow-go years."

- Activity may slow down.
- Travel and hobbies decrease, but medical needs increase.
- Spending may stabilise or slightly decline, especially in discretionary categories.

3. Late Retirement (Ages ~85+)

Also known as the "no-go years."

- Health concerns dominate.
- Long-term care, home assistance, or assisted living becomes a priority.
- Medical and care-related spending often spikes.

Understanding this curve helps in planning for when and where your money will be most needed. Assuming uniform spending across all years is unrealistic, and dangerous.

Cultural and Geographic Considerations

Retirement spending varies by region, culture, and individual values. In some cultures, retirees are expected to live with family, lowering costs. In others, independence is the norm, with retirees responsible for their full living and medical expenses.

Rural vs. Urban Retirement

- **Urban retirees** may face higher housing and living costs but have better access to services.
- **Rural retirees** may have lower costs but more limited access to healthcare and social activities, sometimes leading to increased transportation or relocation expenses.

Living Abroad

Many retirees relocate to countries with a lower cost of living. While this can stretch retirement savings, it can also come with hidden costs:

- Health insurance for expats
- Legal fees or visa requirements
- Exchange rate volatility
- Travel costs to visit family

Planning should account for these potential changes, not just the "cheaper" day-to-day lifestyle.

Psychological and Emotional Factors

The assumption that you'll spend less is often tied to an idea of "slowing down" or becoming less materialistic with age. But that doesn't always align with reality.

- **Boredom leads to spending**: Many retirees fill time with shopping, travel, or experiences.
- **Guilt or generosity**: Retirees often feel compelled to help family or give to causes.
- **Fear of missing out**: Wanting to experience life while still healthy may lead to front-loaded spending.

Ignoring these emotional drivers in your retirement budget sets you up for surprise, and strain.

Planning for Realistic Spending

To avoid being caught off guard, build a retirement plan around your actual lifestyle goals, not abstract assumptions. Here's how:

1. Track Current Expenses Closely

Create a baseline understanding of where your money goes today. This helps identify which costs will change, and which won't.

2. Create a Retirement-Specific Budget

Base it on the three retirement phases:

- Early (active years): more for travel, hobbies, gifts
- Middle: balanced spending
- Late: increase healthcare and home assistance costs

3. Factor in Inflation

Use a reasonable inflation estimate (often 2–4%) to adjust future costs. Remember that healthcare and education (for grandkids or support) often inflate faster than general prices.

4. Plan for Major Expenses

Don't ignore large one-time or recurring costs:

- Replacing a car
- Home repairs
- Family emergencies
- Bucket-list travel

5. Account for Longevity

People are living longer across much of the world. Plan for at least 25–30 years of retirement, especially if you retire in your early 60s or younger.

What If You Didn't Plan for This?

If you're nearing retirement and realising you may spend more than expected, all is not lost. Consider the following strategies:

- **Delay retirement**: Each year you work adds savings and reduces withdrawal pressure.
- **Phase into retirement**: Part-time or freelance work can supplement income.
- **Downsize intentionally**: Sell unnecessary property, vehicles, or assets that cost more than they return.
- **Relocate**: Consider lower-cost regions, domestically or abroad, with careful research.
- **Cut gradually**: Eliminate unnecessary expenses now to build frugal habits.

Our Thoughts on Frugality

Since retiring, our relationship with money has shifted. We're more mindful of our spending, not out of fear, but out of respect for our resources. We

> still enjoy life's luxuries, like travel or dining out, but only with careful planning. Every vacation is budgeted, and we aim to clear our credit cards monthly. We're not frugal to the point of denial, but we're deliberate. The key is knowing where our money goes and spending with intention. It's not about sacrifice, it's about making every dollar count toward a life we enjoy.

Final Thoughts on Financial Control

Retirement should be a time of security and fulfilment, not worry. But assumptions, especially about spending, can quietly sabotage even the most disciplined savers.

The idea that "you'll spend less" is appealing, but it's often not true, at least not uniformly. It's more accurate to say that you'll spend differently, and potentially more during certain periods.

A sound retirement plan isn't built on hopeful assumptions. It's built on honesty, flexibility, and careful consideration of the life you want to live, not just the one you can afford if everything goes perfectly.

The truth? You might spend more in retirement. And if you do, it shouldn't be a problem, as long as you have planned for it.

What Comes After the Finish Line?

For decades, the word retirement has conjured images of well-earned rest: a sun-drenched beach, quiet mornings, leisurely hobbies, or spontaneous travel. It's often seen as the reward for a lifetime of hard work, a destination.

But what if retirement isn't the finish line? What if it's a major transition, not an end?

Across the globe, as people live longer and retire healthier, a surprising challenge has emerged: many retirees don't know what to do next. They have planned meticulously for their finances but haven't thought about how they'll spend their days, where they'll find meaning, or what gives them purpose outside of work.

In this chapter, we explore the profound, and often underestimated, danger of entering retirement without a plan for what comes next. While the financial foundation of retirement is critical, the emotional, psychological, and social blueprint is just as vital to a fulfilling second act.

The New Reality of Retirement

In the past, retirement was relatively brief. In many countries, life expectancy at retirement age was only a few years beyond the retirement threshold. Today, thanks to medical advancements, improved standards of living, and access to healthcare, people can expect to live 20 to 30 years or more after leaving full-time work.

This means that retirement is no longer a short "winding down" period. It's a significant phase of life, a third act, that demands its own vision, goals, and structure.

And yet, many enter retirement with only vague notions of how they'll spend their time. The result? Boredom, isolation, depression, and even health deterioration, all stemming from a lack of direction.

The Psychological Impact of Retirement

In all cultures, work plays a central role in identity. Whether you're a farmer in Kenya, a teacher in Germany, or an entrepreneur in Brazil, what you do is often closely tied to who you are. Retirement disrupts that identity.

Common emotional and psychological challenges include:

- **Loss of identity**: Without a job title, role, or regular responsibilities, some retirees feel invisible or irrelevant.
- **Depression or anxiety**: A lack of routine or purpose can lead to emotional decline.
- **Marital tension**: Couples may struggle to adjust to new rhythms, especially when both partners retire simultaneously.
- **Loneliness and isolation**: Leaving the workplace can mean losing regular social interaction.

These issues don't discriminate by geography or income. Whether you retire in a bustling Asian metropolis or a quiet village in Eastern Europe, the human need for purpose, connection, and meaning remains the same.

What People Think Retirement Will Be Like

Retirement is often idealised, but the reality can be jarring without intentional preparation.

Myth	Reality
"I'll finally relax all the time."	Constant relaxation can lead to boredom and apathy.
"I'll travel endlessly."	Travel can be expensive, tiring, or limited by health.
"I'll take up hobbies."	Many discover they lack the passion or structure to do so.
"I'll enjoy doing nothing."	The novelty of doing nothing wears off quickly.
"It'll feel like a vacation."	Vacations are fun because they end, retirement doesn't.

Planning for retirement isn't just about avoiding negative outcomes; it's about designing a life that excites you.

The Risk of Drifting: What Happens Without a Plan

Let's explore what happens when retirees enter this phase of life without a clear plan for their time, energy, and purpose:

1. Boredom and Restlessness

Many retirees initially enjoy the freedom of retirement. But after a few months, they begin to feel aimless. Without deadlines, meetings, or goals, the days can start to blend.

Boredom isn't just uncomfortable. It can be dangerous. Studies in multiple countries link prolonged boredom with increased risk of:

- Cognitive decline
- Substance abuse
- Depression

2. Erosion of Social Networks

Work provides natural social contact: colleagues, clients, meetings, and team events. Without this, many retirees struggle to maintain relationships. If friendships were mostly workplace-based, they may fade quickly after retirement.

In regions where community gathering spaces or senior programs are lacking, this isolation can become acute.

3. Health Deterioration

Retirees without a routine or goals are more likely to neglect their health. Physical activity may decrease, and regular eating or sleep patterns can become irregular.

Mental health also suffers. Studies from Australia to Scandinavia consistently show that purpose-driven retirees are physically and emotionally healthier.

4. Regret and Loss of Direction

Some retirees feel deep disappointment months or years into retirement. They may ask:

- "Is this it?"
- "Did I waste my potential?"
- "What am I supposed to do now?"

Without a new direction, some may even attempt to re-enter the workforce, not for money, but for meaning.

The Global Face of "What's Next?"

Let's look at how different cultures approach the "what's next" phase, and what we can learn from them.

Japan

In Japanese culture, the idea of ikigai, one's reason for being, is central to a fulfilling life. It exists at the intersection of:

- What you love
- What you're good at
- What the world needs
- What you can be paid for

For retirees, discovering a new *ikigai* can transform their experience of aging. It may involve mentoring, community gardening, or volunteering.

Latin America

In many Latin cultures, elders are integrated into daily life and family structure. They may not be "retired" in a Western sense but take on new roles, caring for grandchildren, managing family businesses, or becoming community leaders.

This continuation of purpose contributes to better mental health outcomes and stronger familial bonds.

Europe

In countries like the Netherlands, Germany, and France, retirees often engage in formal lifelong learning programs. Universities of the Third Age (U3A) or similar models offer courses, workshops, and social events to keep retirees mentally and socially engaged.

This keeps the mind sharp and the social circle vibrant.

Africa and South Asia

In many African and South Asian communities, elders are seen as knowledge keepers and spiritual or practical advisors. Even without formal employment, they continue to hold respected roles in governance, tradition, and education.

How to Build Your "What's Next" Plan

Designing your post-retirement life should be just as intentional as building your financial plan. Here's a framework to help:

1. Define Your Purpose

Purpose doesn't have to be grand; it just needs to be meaningful to you.

Ask yourself:

- What activities energise me?
- What legacy do I want to leave?
- Who or what needs me now?

It could be mentoring, creating art, participating in your faith community, or preserving local history.

2. Create a Daily and Weekly Routine

Without structure, time can feel endless, and empty.

Build a balanced routine that includes:

- Physical activity (walks, yoga, dance, etc.)
- Social interaction
- Intellectual stimulation (reading, courses)
- Leisure and rest
- Treat your calendar as your ally, not your enemy.

3. Explore New Identities

Let go of labels like “teacher,” “engineer,” or “manager.” Begin exploring who you are beyond your job. Try roles like:

- Volunteer
- Artist
- Traveler
- Storyteller
- Mentor

Allow yourself the freedom to grow into something new.

4. Prioritise Connection

Loneliness is one of the biggest health risks in retirement. Build regular touchpoints:

- Join local clubs, spiritual communities, or online interest groups
- Volunteer in causes you care about
- Reach out to old friends regularly
- Stay connected, even if your network has changed.

5. Make Room for Reinvention

Retirement offers a unique opportunity to start over. Many retirees:

- Start small businesses
- Write books or blogs
- Learn new languages
- Teach or tutor
- Travel intentionally (cultural exchange, slow travel, pilgrimage)

View retirement not as the end, but a fresh beginning.

Personal Reflections:

Isabel (Philippines): From Banker to Organic Farmer

After 30 years in finance, Isabel moved to the countryside and began cultivating organic vegetables. She sells her produce locally and mentors' young farmers. "I feel more useful now than I did in the boardroom," she says.

Peter (UK): Lifelong Learner

Peter, a retired civil servant, enrolled in art history and literature classes through a university's retirement program. "I wake up excited again," he says. "I'm not slowing down, I'm finally catching up with the life I postponed."

Rajan (India): Community Educator

Rajan spends his retirement teaching math to underprivileged children in Delhi. "I no longer earn a salary, but I've never felt richer," he says.

Common Obstacles, and How to Overcome Them

1. "I don't know what I want to do."

Start by experimenting. Try small things: a class, a volunteer shift, a new routine. Discovery happens through action, not daydreaming.

2. "I feel guilty relaxing."

Retirement is your time. You don't have to earn rest, you've already earned it. Balance productivity with joy.

3. "I don't have the energy."

You might not need more energy, just more motivation. A sense of purpose naturally fuels action. Start small.

The Greatest Risk Is Doing Nothing

Financial experts often talk about inflation, healthcare costs, and longevity risk. But one of the most underestimated risks in retirement is *em*otional drift, living without direction, without excitement, and without purpose.

This is not a financial issue, it's a life quality issue. You have decades ahead. What will you do with them?

Final Thought: Design the Life You Want

You planned for your retirement fund. You tracked your expenses. You thought about where to live. Now it's time to ask the most important questions of all:

- What will you do with your newfound freedom?

Failing to Plan for Taxes

When most people imagine retirement, they envision a lifestyle filled with relaxation, freedom, and the ability to enjoy the fruits of decades of labour. The last thing on their minds is taxes. Unfortunately, failing to plan for taxes in retirement is a globally widespread oversight that can significantly erode a retiree's income. This chapter will explore the global landscape of retirement taxation, the risks of poor planning, and practical strategies to help you navigate this complex terrain no matter where you live.

The Myth: Retirement Means Lower Taxes

One of the most common assumptions among future retirees is that they will automatically be in a lower tax bracket once they stop working. While it's true that earned income usually decreases in retirement, what many fail to consider is how various forms of retirement income, government pensions, private pensions, investment earnings, real estate income, and even annuity payouts, are still subject to taxation. In some cases, these taxes can be even more burdensome than during one's working years, especially when not planned for in advance.

Let's break down why this misconception is so dangerous and how it plays out across different regions.

Retirement Income Sources and Their Tax Implications

Government and State Pensions

Almost every country offers some form of government pension. However, the taxation of these pensions varies significantly:

- **United States**: Social Security benefits are taxable if your combined income exceeds specific thresholds.
- **Canada**: Old Age Security (OAS) and Canada Pension Plan (CPP) benefits are taxable.
- **United Kingdom**: State Pension is taxable income.
- **Australia**: Age Pension is generally tax-free, but it affects eligibility for other benefits.
- **Germany**: Pensions are partially taxable depending on the year of retirement.
- **India**: Government pensions are mostly taxable unless exempted.

Private and Employer Pensions

These are nearly always considered taxable income. In countries like the U.S., Canada, and the UK, private pensions are taxed as ordinary income. Even in emerging markets, such as South Africa or Brazil, employer pensions are taxed unless special exemptions apply.

Investment Income

Dividends, interest, and capital gains may or may not be taxed, depending on local regulations and whether the income is sourced domestically or internationally. For example:

- **U.S.**: Qualified dividends and long-term capital gains are taxed at reduced rates.
- **India**: Long-term capital gains over a certain threshold are taxed.
- **Germany and France**: Investment income is subject to a flat tax.
- **Australia**: Capital gains tax applies, with a discount for assets held over a year.
- **Japan**: Dividends and capital gains are taxed, often at a flat rate.

Real Estate Income

Rental income is almost universally taxable, though deductions for maintenance, property taxes, and depreciation vary widely.

The Hidden Risks of Poor Tax Planning

Loss of Government Benefits

Many retirees assume their state pension is safe and secure. However, once you begin drawing income from other sources, you may surpass the income thresholds for means-tested benefits, resulting in clawbacks or disqualification. This is common in countries with progressive benefit systems like Canada, the UK, and Australia.

Tax Bracket Creep

Retirees often find themselves pushed into higher tax brackets because they're withdrawing from multiple income sources simultaneously. For example, taking a lump-sum pension payout and selling an investment in the same year could cause a significant tax spike.

Required Withdrawals

Many countries require retirees to begin withdrawing from tax-deferred accounts by a certain age:

- **U.S.**: Required Minimum Distributions (RMDs) begin at age 73.
- **Canada**: Registered Retirement Income Funds (RRIFs) mandate minimum withdrawals.
- **UK**: While there's flexibility, annuity purchases can be irreversible and tax-triggering.

These forced withdrawals can lead to unexpected tax bills and reduced retirement flexibility.

Double Taxation

Retiring abroad or holding international assets without understanding tax treaties can result in double taxation. U.S. citizens, for example, must file U.S. taxes regardless of residency. Countries like Germany or India have treaties that help, but ignorance of them can be costly.

Case Studies from Around the Globe

Maria, Spain

Maria retired at 65 with a pension and rental income from a property she inherited. Initially, her taxes were manageable. But after selling her property for a substantial gain, she owed thousands in capital gains tax, which reduced her annual income and eligibility for senior subsidies.

Anil, India

Anil retired from a government job and assumed his pension was tax-free. It wasn't. Since he also had fixed deposit interest and mutual fund income, he ended up in a higher tax bracket than expected, eroding much of his savings.

Paul, Canada

Paul planned carefully, but didn't anticipate the OAS clawback triggered by RRIF withdrawals. He lost nearly $5,000 per year in benefits simply by not timing his withdrawals better.

Jean, France

Jean retired abroad in Portugal, assuming he'd pay less tax there. Unfortunately, he didn't realise France would still tax his pensions and had to pay in both countries until he got professional help.

Global Tax-Efficient Strategies

While tax laws differ worldwide, the principles of tax-efficient retirement planning are surprisingly universal. Here are strategies that work across borders:

1. Diversify Income Sources by Tax Treatment

Create a mix of income types:

- **Taxable**: Rental income, non-tax-advantaged investments.
- **Tax-deferred**: Traditional retirement accounts (e.g., RRSP, IRA).

- **Tax-free**: Roth accounts, TFSA, ISAs, PPFs, or municipal bonds.

This diversification allows retirees to draw income strategically based on current tax brackets and benefit thresholds.

2. Optimise Withdrawals

Plan your withdrawals to avoid bracket creep. This may include:

- Taking small withdrawals early to reduce large mandatory withdrawals later.
- Using capital gains timing to spread income over multiple years.
- Harvesting losses to offset gains.

3. Use Tax-Advantaged Accounts to Their Full Potential

Each country has tools to encourage retirement savings. Understanding and using them properly is crucial:

- **U.S.**: Roth IRAs, HSAs.
- **Canada**: TFSA, RRSP.
- **UK**: ISAs, SIPP.
- **India**: NPS, PPF.
- **Australia**: Superannuation tax advantages.

Contribute during high-income years, and withdraw in retirement when your tax rate is lower.

4. Don't Forget Health-Related Tax Planning

Healthcare costs often rise in retirement and may be tax-deductible in many countries. Plan for this by tracking expenses and keeping documentation. In the U.S., HSA funds can be used tax-free for medical costs. In India, senior citizens receive higher deductions for health insurance.

5. Plan for International Tax Implications

If you plan to retire abroad or have international assets:

- Understand your home country's exit tax rules.
- Investigate tax treaties between the two nations.
- Consider foreign tax credits or exclusions.

For example, a U.S. expat in Portugal can often exclude foreign-earned income but must plan carefully for passive income like pensions and investments.

Our Story - International Pensions

As British emigrants now living in Canada, we found ourselves navigating pensions from both countries—UK and Canadian government and workplace schemes. At first, it was confusing. Should we consolidate everything in Canada or keep some funds in the UK? Exchange rates added complexity, with the potential to either boost or diminish our income significantly. In the end, we took a balanced approach: we transferred some pensions to Canada and left others in the UK. This strategy worked well for us, but only because we took the time to research, seek advice, and plan carefully.

Professional Help

Tax laws are complex and change frequently. While it's important to educate yourself, working with a tax professional who understands retirement planning is invaluable. In cross-border cases, seek advisors with international tax expertise.

Questions to ask a tax planner:

- How is my pension taxed?
- Are my withdrawals timed for efficiency?
- Am I triggering unnecessary taxes?
- What deductions or credits can I take advantage of?

Summary

If you ignore taxes in retirement, you risk shrinking your wealth faster than you planned. Yet with thoughtful, proactive planning, taxes can be minimised and managed.

Retirement isn't just about saving money. It's about keeping it.

By understanding your country's tax policies, using tax-advantaged accounts, diversifying income, and planning withdrawals carefully, you protect your retirement lifestyle. Remember, taxes may be certain, but how much you pay is not.

Neglecting Estate and Legacy Planning

Retirement planning often focuses on finances, saving enough, investing wisely, and budgeting for post-work life. But one area that is frequently overlooked, yet critically important, is estate and legacy planning. Around the globe, people of all income levels underestimate the impact of failing to make a clear plan for their estate. Whether you're in the United States, India, the United Kingdom, Australia, South Africa, or elsewhere, neglecting estate and legacy planning can jeopardise not just your peace of mind, but also your family's future and the legacy you wish to leave behind.

What Is Estate and Legacy Planning?

Estate planning is the process of arranging, during your lifetime, for the management and disposal of your estate after your death. It ensures that your assets are distributed according to your wishes, taxes are minimised, and potential family conflicts are avoided.

Legacy planning goes beyond the financial and legal aspects. It encompasses the values, memories, charitable intentions, and cultural heritage you wish to pass on to future generations. It's about crafting a long-term impact that aligns with your life's principles.

Together, estate and legacy planning create a holistic approach to ensuring your life's work continues to benefit your loved ones and community after you're gone.

Global Myths and Misconceptions

1. "I'm not rich enough to need estate planning."

Estate planning isn't only for the wealthy. Even modest estates can cause significant complications without clear direction. In many countries, dying without a will (intestate) leads to long, expensive legal processes and unintended inheritance outcomes.

2. "My family knows what I want."

Wishes not legally documented are not binding. Emotional disagreements among family members are common, especially in the absence of a clear, written plan. Legal documents remove ambiguity.

3. "It's a one-time task."

Estate planning is dynamic. As life evolves, marriage, divorce, children, property acquisitions, so should your estate plan.

4. "Estate laws are the same everywhere."

Laws vary significantly. In France, forced heirship laws dictate a portion of inheritance. In India, different religious personal laws govern inheritance. In the U.S., estate taxes and probate differ state by state.

The Consequences of Not Planning

1. Family Conflict

When there's no clear will or legal structure, disputes over property, heirship, and responsibilities can arise. These conflicts are not just financially damaging; they often permanently fracture relationships.

2. Government Intervention

In the absence of a will, the state often decides how assets are divided. In many countries, intestacy laws override personal wishes. This can mean estranged relatives inherit over close friends or caregivers.

3. Tax Burden

In countries like the United Kingdom and the United States, large estates may be subject to estate or inheritance taxes. Without careful planning, heirs may be forced to sell assets to cover tax bills.

4. Delays and Legal Fees

Probate, the legal process of administering an estate, can take months or years, delaying the transfer of assets. Legal costs can reduce the value of your estate substantially.

5. Unprotected Minor Children or Dependents

Failing to appoint guardians for minor children or dependents with special needs can leave their future in uncertainty.

Core Elements of a Global Estate Plan

1. **Will (Last Will and Testament)**
    - Designates asset distribution
    - Names guardians for minor children
    - Must comply with local laws

2. **Power of Attorney (POA)**
    - Authorises someone to act on your behalf in financial or legal matters if you become incapacitated
    - In some countries, different documents are needed for financial and healthcare decisions
3. **Healthcare Directive (Living Will)**
    - Details your medical care preferences if you are unable to communicate
    - Called an Advanced Directive in the U.S., and an Advance Decision in the UK
4. **Trusts**
    - Useful for bypassing probate, managing multi-country assets, and providing ongoing support to dependents
    - Revocable and irrevocable trusts serve different purposes depending on tax planning and control needs
5. **Beneficiary Designations**
    - Bank accounts, insurance policies, and retirement accounts often allow for direct beneficiary designation, which overrides wills
6. **Digital Legacy**
    - Includes access to online accounts, digital currency wallets, and social media. Many platforms now offer legacy planning tools

Special Considerations by Region

United States

- Federal estate tax exemption is high, but varies by state
- Revocable living trusts are common to avoid probate
- Durable Power of Attorney and Healthcare Proxy are vital

United Kingdom

- Inheritance tax (IHT) is 40% on estates over a certain threshold
- Trusts and gifting can reduce IHT liability
- Property ownership affects how inheritance is passed on

India

- Laws differ by religion (Hindu Succession Act, Muslim Personal Law, etc.)
- Wills are recommended even for small estates
- Digital wills are emerging but still legally contested

Australia

- No federal estate tax, but capital gains tax can apply upon inheritance
- Testamentary trusts are common to provide tax benefits to heirs

Canada

- No estate tax, but final tax return includes capital gains on deemed dispositions
- Probate fees vary by province

South Africa

- Estate duty applies above a certain threshold
- Capital Gains Tax can apply upon death
- Wills must be clear and comply with formal requirements

Middle East

- In many Gulf Cooperation Council (GCC) countries, Sharia law may apply by default
- Expats should register wills locally or in their home country depending on residency status

Planning for Cross-Border Families

Global families must address multiple legal systems.

Issues include:

- Double taxation
- Recognition of foreign wills
- Managing properties across jurisdictions

Solutions:

- Use of international trusts
- Dual wills (one for each country, carefully drafted to avoid conflicts)
- Legal counsel familiar with cross-border estate planning

Legacy Planning

Legacy is about your life's values and how they continue beyond your lifetime. Consider these legacy components:

1. Philanthropy and Charitable Giving

Donor-advised funds, charitable trusts, and direct bequests are ways to leave a lasting impact. Choose causes that reflect your beliefs.

2. Heir Education

Ensure your heirs are financially literate. Family meetings, ethical wills (non-legal documents expressing your values), and mentorship are effective tools.

3. Cultural Preservation

Pass down traditions, stories, recipes, and cultural practices through recorded histories, books, or family archives.

4. Environmental Legacies

Sustainable investments and green trusts support eco-conscious wealth transfer.

Steps to Get Started

1. **Take Inventory**
    - List assets, debts, insurance policies, and digital accounts
2. **Choose Executors and Guardians**
    - Pick reliable, trustworthy individuals. Ensure they understand your intentions

3. **Consult Professionals**
    - Work with estate lawyers, financial advisors, and tax experts familiar with your country's legal system
4. **Review Regularly**
    - Update after major life events (marriage, divorce, births, deaths, relocation)
5. **Communicate Clearly**
    - Share your plan with your family to prevent confusion and build understanding

Final Thoughts

Retirement should be a time of peace and fulfilment, not anxiety about what happens next. A complete retirement plan includes thoughtful estate and legacy planning, regardless of your net worth or location.

You've worked hard to build your life. Now ensure it endures in the way you want. Empower your family, support the causes you care about, and create a legacy that reflects the values you hold dear.

Embracing New Horizons

Retirement is often viewed as a time of rest and relaxation, a well-deserved break after decades of hard work. However, it can also be a vibrant chapter filled with new experiences, personal growth, and the pursuit of passions that may have been set aside during the busyness of career life. One of the most fulfilling ways to embrace this new phase is through hobbies. Hobbies not only provide enjoyment but also contribute to mental, emotional, and physical well-being. In this chapter, we will explore a variety of hobbies that retirees can take up, each offering unique benefits and opportunities for personal enrichment.

1. The Importance of Hobbies in Retirement

Before diving into specific hobbies, it's essential to understand why engaging in activities during retirement is crucial. Hobbies can:

Enhance Mental Health: Engaging in enjoyable activities can reduce stress, anxiety, and depression. They provide a sense of purpose and accomplishment, which is vital for mental well-being.

Promote Physical Health: Many hobbies involve physical activity, which can help maintain mobility, strength, and overall health. Regular movement is essential for preventing age-related decline.

Encourage Social Connections: Hobbies often provide opportunities to meet new people and build friendships, combating loneliness and isolation that can sometimes accompany retirement.

Stimulate Creativity: Many hobbies encourage creative expression, which can be incredibly fulfilling and can lead to personal growth and self-discovery.

Provide Lifelong Learning: Retirement is an excellent time to learn new skills or deepen existing knowledge. Hobbies can be a gateway to continuous education and personal development.

With these benefits in mind, let's explore a diverse array of hobbies that retirees can consider.

2. Creative Pursuits

2.1 Painting and Drawing

Artistic expression through painting or drawing can be incredibly therapeutic. Whether you're a beginner or have some experience, the act of creating can be a joyful and fulfilling endeavour. Local community centres often offer classes for all skill levels, and online tutorials can provide guidance and inspiration.

2.2 Writing

Writing can take many forms, from journaling and blogging to poetry and fiction. It's a powerful way to express thoughts and feelings, document life experiences, or even share stories with others. Joining a writing group can provide motivation and constructive feedback.

2.3 Photography

Photography encourages you to see the world through a different lens, literally. It can be a wonderful way to capture memories, explore nature, or document family events. Many retirees find joy in taking classes to improve their skills or joining photography clubs to share their work.

2.4 Crafting

Crafting encompasses a wide range of activities, including knitting, crocheting, scrapbooking, pottery and woodworking. These hands-on hobbies can be incredibly satisfying and allow for the creation of personalised gifts or home decor. Crafting can also be a social activity, with many groups meeting to share ideas and techniques.

3. Physical Activities

3.1 Gardening

Gardening is not only a rewarding hobby but also a great way to stay active. Whether you have a large backyard or a small balcony, growing flowers, vegetables, or herbs can bring joy and a sense of accomplishment. Gardening also connects you with nature, which has numerous mental health benefits.

3.2 Walking and Hiking

Walking is one of the simplest and most accessible forms of exercise. It can be done almost anywhere and is a great way to explore your local area. For those who enjoy nature, hiking can provide a more adventurous experience, allowing you to discover beautiful landscapes and wildlife.

3.3 Yoga and Tai Chi

Both yoga and tai chi focus on gentle movements, balance, and mindfulness. They are excellent for improving flexibility, strength, and mental clarity. Many community centres and gyms offer classes specifically designed for seniors, making it easy to get started.

3.4 Dancing

Dancing is a fun way to stay active and socialise. Whether you prefer ballroom, line dancing, or salsa, there are classes available for all skill levels. Dancing not only provides physical benefits but also boosts mood and cognitive function.

4. Intellectual Engagement

4.1 Reading

Reading is a timeless hobby that can transport you to different worlds, expand your knowledge, and stimulate your imagination. Joining a book club can enhance the experience by providing opportunities for discussion and social interaction.

4.2 Learning a New Language

Learning a new language can be a challenging yet rewarding endeavour. It keeps the mind sharp and opens up new cultural experiences. Many online platforms and local community colleges offer language courses tailored for seniors.

4.3 Playing Musical Instruments

If you've always wanted to learn an instrument, retirement is the perfect time to pursue that dream. Whether it's the piano, guitar, or even a wind instrument, playing music can be incredibly fulfilling. Many community centres offer lessons for beginners.

4.4 Puzzles and Games

Engaging in puzzles, such as crosswords, Sudoku, or jigsaw puzzles, can be a great way to keep your mind sharp. These activities challenge cognitive skills and can be enjoyed alone or with friends and family. Board games and card games also provide social interaction and can be a fun way to spend time with loved ones.

Our Story - Hobbies

Retirement gave me the freedom to fully immerse myself in both lifelong passions and new pursuits. Reading has always been a great joy for me, and with more time on my hands, I now read more widely, exploring genres and authors I once overlooked. This naturally led to writing, something I'd dabbled in over the years, but never seriously pursued until retirement. This book is my 12th, and I plan to continue writing for as long as readers are willing to turn the pages.

Wanting to improve my craft, I returned to university to study creative writing. It was both challenging and deeply rewarding, helping me refine my voice and style. While there, I enrolled in a pottery elective, something I'd never considered before. To my surprise, it quickly became another passion. Now, I attend regular pottery classes and enjoy creating functional art for our home.

As I've mentioned previously, travel remains a big part of our lives. We're currently planning our next vacation, and this time it will be longer, giving us a chance to truly settle in at the vacation site, and experience a new place at a slower pace.

Back home, I've taken on a major personal project: completing our unfinished basement. It's a labour of love, with plans to add extra bedrooms and a bathroom. The work is physical and satisfying, a perfect counterbalance to my quieter, creative interests.

Since retiring, I've found myself busier than ever. The key, I believe, is planning. Before I left work, I thought carefully about how I wanted to spend my time. I didn't drift into retirement; I

> stepped into it with purpose. That made all the difference.

5. Community Involvement

5.1 Volunteering

Volunteering is a fulfilling way to give back to the community while also meeting new people. There are countless opportunities available, from working with local charities and non-profits to mentoring youth or helping at animal shelters. Volunteering not only benefits others but can also provide a sense of purpose and fulfilment.

5.2 Joining Clubs and Organisations

Many communities have clubs and organisations that cater to various interests, from book clubs and gardening groups to travel clubs and sports leagues. Joining these groups can help you connect with like-minded individuals and foster new friendships.

5.3 Attending Workshops and Classes

Many local community centres, libraries, and colleges offer workshops and classes on a wide range of topics. Whether you're interested in cooking, photography, or technology, these classes can provide valuable skills and opportunities to meet new people.

6. Travel and Exploration

6.1 Local Exploration

Retirement is an excellent time to explore your local area. Visit museums, parks, historical sites, and local attractions that you may have overlooked during your working years. Many communities offer guided tours that can provide new insights into familiar places.

6.2 Traveling Abroad

If you have the means and desire, traveling abroad can be one of the most enriching experiences of retirement. Whether it's a road trip across the country or an international adventure, travel allows you to experience new cultures, cuisines, and landscapes. Consider joining travel groups designed for seniors, which can provide companionship and safety.

6.3 Staycations

If travel isn't feasible, consider a staycation. Explore nearby attractions, try new restaurants, or indulge in local activities. A staycation can be just as refreshing and exciting as traveling far from home.

7. Technology and Digital Hobbies

7.1 Blogging or Vlogging

If you enjoy writing or speaking, consider starting a blog or vlog. Share your experiences, hobbies, or expertise with a wider audience. This can be a creative outlet and a way to connect with others who share your interests.

7.2 Social Media Engagement

Social media platforms can help you stay connected with family and friends, share your hobbies, and discover new interests. Learning to navigate these platforms can also be a fun challenge and a way to engage with the digital world.

7.3 Online Courses

The internet is a treasure trove of knowledge. Websites like Coursera, Udemy, and Khan Academy offer a wide range of online courses on various subjects.

Whether you want to learn about history, science, or a new skill, there's likely a course available to suit your interests.

8. Mindfulness and Relaxation

8.1 Meditation

Meditation is a practice that can enhance mental clarity, reduce stress, and promote emotional well-being. There are many forms of meditation, from guided sessions to mindfulness practices. Consider joining a local meditation group or using apps to get started.

8.2 Tai Chi and Qigong

These ancient Chinese practices combine gentle movements with mindfulness and breathing techniques. They are excellent for improving balance, flexibility, and overall well-being. Many community centres offer classes specifically designed for seniors.

8.3 Nature Walks

Spending time in nature has been shown to reduce stress and improve mood. Consider taking regular walks in local parks or nature reserves. The sights and sounds of nature can be incredibly calming and rejuvenating.

9. Culinary Adventures

9.1 Cooking and Baking

Retirement is a great time to experiment in the kitchen. Try new recipes, explore different cuisines, or take cooking classes. Baking can also be a fun and rewarding hobby, allowing you to create delicious treats for yourself and others.

9.2 Wine or Beer Tasting

If you enjoy beverages, consider exploring the world of wine or craft beer. Many local wineries and breweries offer tastings and tours, providing an opportunity to learn about the production process and sample different varieties.

9.3 Gardening for Food

If you have a green thumb, consider starting a vegetable or herb garden. Growing your own food can be incredibly satisfying and allows you to enjoy fresh produce right from your backyard.

10. Crafting and DIY Projects

10.1 Home Improvement Projects

Retirement can be an excellent time to tackle home improvement projects you've been putting off. Whether it's painting a room, redecorating, or building furniture, these projects can be fulfilling and enhance your living space.

10.2 Upcycling and Repurposing

Get creative by upcycling and repurposing items around your home. This hobby not only helps reduce waste but also allows you to create unique decor or functional items. From turning old furniture into new treasures to crafting art from discarded materials, the possibilities are endless.

10.3 Sewing and Quilting

Sewing and quilting can be incredibly rewarding hobbies that allow you to create beautiful and practical items. Whether you're making clothes, home decor, or quilts, these crafts can be both relaxing and productive.

Many community centres offer classes for beginners, and there are countless online resources to help you get started.

11. Animal Companionship

11.1 Pet Ownership

If you love animals, consider adopting a pet. Dogs and cats can provide companionship, reduce stress, and encourage physical activity. Caring for a pet can also give you a sense of purpose and routine. If you're not ready for the commitment of pet ownership, consider volunteering at a local animal shelter.

11.2 Animal Training

If you already have a pet, consider taking up animal training as a hobby. Training your dog or teaching your cat new tricks can be a fun way to bond with your pet while also providing mental stimulation for both of you. Many local trainers offer classes, or you can find resources online.

12. Exploring New Cultures

12.1 Cultural Events and Festivals

Many communities host cultural events and festivals that celebrate diversity through food, music, art, and dance. Attending these events can be a fun way to learn about different cultures and meet new people. Look for local calendars or community boards to find upcoming events.

12.2 Cooking Classes

If you're interested in exploring different cuisines, consider taking cooking classes that focus on international dishes. This can be a fun way to learn new skills while also enjoying delicious food. Many culinary schools and community centres offer classes for all skill levels.

12.3 Language Exchange

If you're learning a new language, consider joining a language exchange group. These groups allow you to practice speaking with native speakers while helping them learn your language. It's a great way to make friends and immerse yourself in a new culture.

13. Adventure and Outdoor Activities

13.1 Birdwatching

Birdwatching is a peaceful and rewarding hobby that allows you to connect with nature. It can be done in your backyard or at local parks and nature reserves. Consider investing in a good pair of binoculars and a field guide to help identify different species.

13.2 Fishing

Fishing can be a relaxing way to spend time outdoors. Whether you prefer freshwater or saltwater fishing, this hobby can provide a sense of tranquillity and connection to nature. Many local fishing clubs offer resources and community events for beginners.

13.3 Camping

If you enjoy the great outdoors, consider taking up camping. It's a wonderful way to disconnect from daily stressors and immerse yourself in nature. Whether you prefer tent camping or RVing, there are countless campgrounds to explore.

14. Building Skills and Knowledge

14.1 DIY Home Repairs

Learning basic home repair skills can be a valuable hobby. From fixing leaky faucets to patching drywall, these skills can save you money and give you a sense of accomplishment. There are many online tutorials and community workshops available to help you get started.

14.2 Car Maintenance

If you have an interest in cars, consider learning basic maintenance skills. Understanding how to change your oil, replace a tire, or perform other simple repairs can be empowering and save you money in the long run.

14.3 Technology Skills

As technology continues to evolve, staying up-to-date can be beneficial. Consider taking classes or online courses to learn about new software, apps, or devices. This knowledge can enhance your daily life and help you stay connected with family and friends.

15. Spiritual and Personal Growth

15.1 Meditation and Mindfulness

Practicing meditation and mindfulness can help you cultivate a sense of peace and presence in your life. There are many resources available, including apps, books, and local classes, to help you get started on your mindfulness journey.

15.2 Journaling

Journaling can be a powerful tool for self-reflection and personal growth. Consider keeping a daily journal to document your thoughts, feelings, and experiences. This practice can help you process emotions and gain insights into your life.

15.3 Attending Workshops and Retreats

Look for workshops or retreats focused on personal development, spirituality, or wellness. These events can provide valuable insights, new perspectives, and opportunities for self-discovery.

16. The Joy of Learning

16.1 Continuing Education

Many colleges and universities offer continuing education programs for seniors. These classes can cover a wide range of topics, from art history to computer science. Engaging in lifelong learning can keep your mind sharp and provide opportunities to meet new people.

16.2 Online Learning Platforms

In addition to traditional continuing education, online learning platforms like Coursera, edX, and Masterclass offer a plethora of courses on various subjects. You can learn at your own pace and explore topics that pique your interest, whether it's philosophy, science, or creative writing. Many of these platforms offer free courses, making it accessible for everyone.

16.3 Community College Classes

Local community colleges often provide affordable classes for seniors. These classes can range from academic subjects to practical skills like cooking, photography, or computer literacy. Enrolling in a community college course can also be a great way to meet people in your area who share similar interests.

17. Embracing Technology

17.1 Digital Photography

With the advent of smartphones and digital cameras, photography has become more accessible than ever. Learning the basics of digital photography can be a rewarding hobby. You can explore different styles, such as portrait, landscape, or macro photography, and even edit your photos using software like Adobe Lightroom or Photoshop.

17.2 Video Editing

If you enjoy capturing moments on video, consider learning video editing. There are many user-friendly software options available, such as iMovie or Adobe Premiere Elements, that allow you to create beautiful videos of your travels, family gatherings, or personal projects. This hobby can also be a great way to share your experiences with family and friends.

17.3 Blogging and Content Creation

If you have a passion for writing or sharing your experiences, consider starting a blog or YouTube channel. This can be a creative outlet and a way to connect with others who share your interests. You can write about your hobbies, travel experiences, or even share tips and advice based on your life experiences.

18. Social Engagement

18.1 Joining a Book Club

Joining a book club can be a fantastic way to engage with literature and meet new people. Many libraries and community centres host book clubs that focus on various genres. This social activity encourages discussion and can introduce you to books you might not have picked up otherwise.

18.2 Game Nights

Organising or participating in game nights can be a fun way to socialise. Whether it's board games, card games, or trivia, these gatherings can foster camaraderie and laughter. Consider inviting friends or neighbours over for a regular game night to strengthen your social connections.

18.3 Group Travel

If you enjoy traveling, consider joining a group travel organisation that caters to seniors. These groups often plan trips that include guided tours, accommodations, and activities, making travel easier and more enjoyable. Traveling with a group can also provide companionship and shared experiences.

19. Exploring the Arts

19.1 Theatre and Performing Arts

Attending local theatre productions, concerts, or dance performances can be a wonderful way to appreciate the arts. Many communities have vibrant arts scenes, and participating in these events can enrich your cultural experiences. Consider volunteering at local theatres or arts organisations to get involved.

19.2 Art Classes

If you have an interest in visual arts, consider taking art classes in painting, drawing, or sculpture. Many community centres and art schools offer classes for all skill levels. This can be a great way to explore your creativity and meet fellow art enthusiasts.

19.3 Music Appreciation

If you love music, consider exploring different genres or learning about music history. You might also enjoy attending concerts or joining a local choir or music group. Engaging with music can be a joyful and enriching experience.

20. The Benefits of Hobbies

20.1 Building Confidence

Engaging in new hobbies can help build confidence and self-esteem. As you learn new skills and overcome challenges, you'll gain a sense of accomplishment that can positively impact other areas of your life.

20.2 Creating a Routine

In retirement, it can be easy to fall into a routine of inactivity. Hobbies provide structure and purpose to your day, helping you create a fulfilling routine that includes activities you enjoy.

20.3 Enhancing Quality of Life

Ultimately, hobbies contribute to a higher quality of life. They provide opportunities for joy, connection, and personal growth. By exploring new interests and passions, you can create a rich and fulfilling retirement experience.

21. Overcoming Barriers to Hobbies

21.1 Time Constraints

While retirement often provides more free time, some retirees may still feel constrained by other responsibilities, such as caregiving or volunteering. It's essential to prioritise your hobbies and carve out time for activities that bring you joy.

21.2 Physical Limitations

If you have physical limitations, consider hobbies that can be adapted to your abilities. Many activities, such as painting, writing, or crafting, can be done while seated or with minimal physical exertion. Look for adaptive classes or resources that cater to your needs.

21.3 Fear of the Unknown

Starting a new hobby can be intimidating, especially if you're worried about your skill level or how you'll be perceived by others. Remember that everyone starts somewhere, and the goal of a hobby is to enjoy the process rather than achieve perfection. Embrace the learning curve, and don't hesitate to seek out beginner classes or groups where you can feel supported and encouraged.

22. Finding Your Passion

22.1 Experimentation

One of the joys of retirement is the freedom to explore various interests without the pressure of deadlines or expectations. Don't be afraid to try out different hobbies until you find what resonates with you. Attend workshops, take classes, or simply dabble in activities that pique your curiosity. You might discover a hidden talent or passion you never knew you had.

22.2 Reflecting on Past Interests

Consider revisiting hobbies you enjoyed in your youth. Whether it was playing a musical instrument, painting, or participating in sports, reconnecting with these activities can reignite your passion and bring back fond memories.

22.3 Seeking Inspiration

Look for inspiration in your surroundings. Attend local art shows, community events, or lectures to spark new ideas. Engaging with others who share your interests can also provide motivation and encouragement to pursue new hobbies.

23. Creating a Supportive Environment

23.1 Setting Up a Dedicated Space

Creating a dedicated space for your hobbies can enhance your enjoyment and productivity. Whether it's a corner of your living room for crafting, a small garden plot, or a cosy reading nook, having a designated area can help you focus and immerse yourself in your activities.

23.2 Involving Family and Friends

Share your hobbies with family and friends. Invite them to join you in activities, whether it's cooking a meal together, attending a class, or going on a hike. Involving loved ones can deepen your connections and make your hobbies even more enjoyable.

23.3 Joining Online Communities

If you're interested in hobbies that may not have local groups, consider joining online communities. Social media platforms, forums, and websites dedicated to specific interests can connect you with like-minded individuals from around the world. These communities can provide support, inspiration, and a sense of belonging.

24. The Journey of Self-Discovery

24.1 Embracing Change

Retirement is a time of transition, and embracing change can lead to personal growth. As you explore new hobbies, you may discover new aspects of yourself and your interests. Be open to the journey and allow yourself to evolve.

24.2 Setting Goals

Setting personal goals related to your hobbies can provide motivation and a sense of direction. Whether it's completing a painting, finishing a book, or mastering a new recipe, having goals can enhance your sense of accomplishment and fulfilment.

24.3 Celebrating Achievements

Take time to celebrate your achievements, no matter how small. Whether it's completing a project, learning a new skill, or simply enjoying the process, acknowledging your progress can boost your confidence and encourage you to continue pursuing your passions.

25. Conclusion

Retirement is a unique opportunity to embrace new experiences, explore passions, and cultivate a fulfilling lifestyle. Hobbies play a vital role in enhancing your quality of life, providing mental stimulation, physical activity, and social connections. By engaging in activities that bring you joy, you can create a vibrant and meaningful retirement.

As you embark on this exciting journey, remember that the key is to enjoy the process. Allow yourself the freedom to explore, learn, and grow. Whether you choose to paint, garden, volunteer, or travel, each hobby has the potential to enrich your life in countless ways. Embrace this new chapter with an open heart and a curious mind, and you'll find that retirement can be one of the most rewarding phases of your life.

In the end, the hobbies you choose to pursue will not only fill your days with joy but will also create lasting memories and connections that will enrich your life for years to come. So, take that first step, dive into your interests, and let the adventure of retirement unfold before you. The world is full of possibilities, and it's never too late to discover what brings you happiness and fulfilment.

Remember – retirees get up in the morning with nothing to do, but go to bed with only half the things done.

The Challenges of Traveling

For many retirees, travel is the dream. After decades of punching clocks, attending meetings, and accruing vacation days that were rarely used, retirement seems like the perfect time to finally explore the world. Whether it's a Mediterranean cruise, a tour through the temples of Southeast Asia, or a campervan trip across North America, the freedom to roam feels like one of the greatest rewards of retirement.

But the truth is, traveling after 65 comes with a unique set of challenges. Travel is a recurring goal, but it often becomes one of the most complex elements to manage. There are hurdles, financial, physical, logistical, and emotional, that many don't expect until they're already on the road (or worse, stuck in an airport).

In this chapter, we'll dive into the specific challenges retirees face while traveling, from navigating international insurance policies to managing medications and maintaining mobility. It's not about discouraging travel. It's about preparing for it with eyes wide open and a plan in hand.

1. The Illusion of Credit Card Insurance Coverage

One of the most common misconceptions among retirees is that their credit card's built-in travel insurance is sufficient. Many premium cards do advertise travel coverage, but there are important limitations:

- **Age Caps**: Most credit card travel insurance policies sharply reduce or eliminate coverage for travellers over 65 or 70. Even if you've used the card to book the trip, you may be uncovered or under-covered once you reach a certain age.
- **Trip Duration Limits**: Credit card policies often only cover trips up to a certain length, usually 15 to 30 days. Planning an extended stay? You may unknowingly be uninsured.
- **Medical Pre-Existing Condition Exclusions**: Many policies have strict clauses excluding coverage for pre-existing conditions or requiring a stability period that can be as long as 6 to 12 months.

The solution? Always read the fine print and don't assume. Supplement your credit card insurance with standalone travel medical insurance specifically tailored for seniors. Companies like Medipac, Blue Cross, and Allianz offer senior-focused plans that can be customised based on your health status and trip length.

2. Medical Coverage Abroad: What Your Home Plan Won't Cover

For most retirees, especially in Canada or the U.S., health care at home is publicly or privately insured to some degree. But the moment you leave the country, coverage may disappear or become limited to reimbursement models that pay out only a fraction of actual costs.

Imagine breaking your leg in Mexico or suffering a heart attack in Portugal. Medical evacuation alone can cost between $25,000 and $100,000. A night in an ICU overseas can rack up bills in the tens of thousands.

If you have existing health conditions, consider:

- Carrying a detailed medical summary from your doctor.
- Packing extra medication in its original packaging, along with a copy of your prescriptions.
- Knowing where nearby hospitals or clinics are, especially if you're traveling to a remote area.
- Researching hospitals that offer English-speaking doctors.

And always buy comprehensive travel health insurance that includes emergency medical coverage, trip interruption, and medical evacuation.

3. The Realities of Mobility and Accessibility

Travel brochures rarely show stairs, uneven sidewalks, or inaccessible public transportation, but those realities exist in many destinations. For retirees with arthritis, joint pain, or mobility aids, getting around can be a challenge.

When planning travel, ask:

- Does your hotel have elevators and walk-in showers?
- Are sidewalks and transit options wheelchair-friendly?
- Can tours or excursions accommodate mobility devices?
- Are long walking distances or cobblestones going to be a problem?

Investing in a collapsible cane, walking poles, or even a lightweight travel wheelchair may make a big difference. Many cities are improving accessibility but do your homework before booking.

Our Story - Travels

We prioritised travel throughout our lives and decided that we would continue to travel through our retirement. Throughout our lives we have visited and enjoyed 42 countries between us, with 31 being together. This number of countries is approximately twenty two percent of all the countries in the world. We have plans to do at least twenty percent more before we are too old to travel anymore. The world is simply too fascinating, too layered in history, flavour, and beauty to stop now.

Since we retired, we have changed how we travel. We are no longer in a rush. Gone are the days of racing through airports to catch connecting flights or squeezing five cities into a weeklong holiday. Now, we savour. We spend more time in each destination, sometimes weeks or even a month. But that slower pace comes with different, updated logistics. We spend more time ensuring we have sufficient insurance for seniors, including robust medical coverage. Peace of mind is priceless.

We invested in NEXUS to ease our way through airport security and immigration. Priority Pass has become our gateway to comfortable lounges, where we rest and refresh before boarding. We also download an e-SIM before every trip and install a reliable translator app. These two simple tools have opened doors for us, turning smiles of confusion into shared laughs with locals. It's amazing what a few words in someone's native language can do.

I take medications daily, so we always travel with a doctor's letter, just in case. I can't stress this enough: be prepared. Research the country's customs and entry requirements thoroughly. What might seem harmless in your home country may be restricted elsewhere. Always ensure you can confidently answer any question at the border. Preparation can mean the difference between a smooth entry and a stressful, even trip-ending experience.

In all our years of travel, we never truly experienced jetlag, until recently. On our last trip, we found ourselves wide awake at 2 a.m. for the first two nights. There we were, sitting in our small hotel room, listening to a coffee machine hum and watching a television programme we couldn't understand. We laughed at ourselves before deciding to get dressed and go for a walk. At that hour, the city had a soul of its own, quiet, reflective, and oddly intimate. We saw bakers unloading fresh bread, street sweepers humming tunes, and the first stirrings of the day.

The moral? Don't waste your time sitting inside if the streets are safe. Get out. See what the city offers in its off-hours. Retirement travel is not about ticking boxes, it's about discovering the world anew, at your own pace, one unhurried morning at a time.

4. Prescription Medications and Customs Rules

Managing prescriptions while traveling internationally is more complicated than many assume. Some countries have strict regulations on medications, even over-the-counter drugs.

For example, certain painkillers or sleeping aids that are legal in the U.S. or Canada may be restricted in countries like Japan, the UAE, or Singapore.

- Keep all medications in original, labelled containers.
- Bring a translated letter from your doctor explaining what each medication is and why it's prescribed.
- Pack at least double the amount you need (in case of delays).
- Don't rely on foreign pharmacies to stock what you need, it's not guaranteed.

And never pack medication in checked luggage. Always carry it in your hand luggage, with your travel insurance details.

5. Travel Fatigue Is Real

Retirees often find they no longer bounce back from jet lag or a long travel day like they used to. Your body's resilience changes with age, and pushing too hard, multiple flights, late nights, long tours, can turn a trip into a burden.

Signs of travel fatigue include:

- Poor sleep and irritability
- Confusion or dizziness
- Increased risk of falls
- Gastrointestinal discomfort
- Elevated blood pressure

Combat this by:

- Scheduling rest days into your itinerary
- Avoiding back-to-back flights or red-eye flights
- Staying hydrated and eating lightly on travel days
- Booking comfortable, direct flights when possible

- Slow travel, spending longer in one place and immersing yourself in the local culture, can be far more fulfilling (and less exhausting) than whirlwind itineraries.

6. Airport Navigation and Security

Modern airports are huge, crowded, and stressful. From security checks to gate changes and luggage claim chaos, the process can be overwhelming, especially for those with physical limitations or cognitive decline.

What you can do:

- Request wheelchair assistance in advance (even if you don't use one daily).
- Use priority lines if you have a medical condition.
- Fly with airlines known for senior-friendly services, like WestJet or Air Canada.
- Consider Global Entry, NEXUS, or TSA PreCheck to reduce wait times.

And don't underestimate the power of traveling with a companion or family member who can manage logistics, especially for longer or multi-leg journeys.

7. The Solo Traveler Challenge

Many retirees, especially women, choose to travel solo. It's empowering and liberating, but it also comes with added risks.

Safety tips for solo senior travellers:

- Book accommodations in safe, central neighbourhoods.
- Avoid arriving in new cities after dark.

- Keep digital and printed copies of your ID and insurance.
- Use apps that share your location with family or friends.
- Enrol in government traveller registration programs (like STEP in the U.S. or ROCA in Canada).

You can also join group travel programs tailored for seniors, offering safety in numbers, social engagement, and curated experiences.

8. Currency, Budgeting, and Digital Payments

Currency exchange and foreign transaction fees can eat into your travel budget fast. Seniors are especially vulnerable to scams, skimming, or using the wrong type of card abroad.

- Use travel credit cards with no foreign transaction fees.
- Notify your bank before departure to avoid frozen accounts.
- Withdraw local cash only from trusted bank ATMs.
- Use currency converter apps to avoid confusion.

Also, beware of dynamic currency conversion scams where a merchant charges you in your home currency at a poor rate. Always choose the local currency when paying with a card.

9. Climate, Time Zones, and Seasonal Risks

Traveling to a hot, humid country when you have respiratory issues, or a mountainous area when managing heart conditions, can pose hidden dangers.

You may need time to acclimate, medication adjustments, or changes in activity levels. Heat stroke, dehydration, and altitude sickness are real concerns for older travellers.

Plan accordingly:

- Travel during mild seasons (spring, early fall)
- Stay hydrated and avoid midday sun exposure
- Allow adjustment days when changing time zones
- Check air quality if you have asthma or COPD

10. Travel Insurance: The Real Fine Print

Not all travel insurance is created equal. Some policies are designed more for lost luggage than medical crises. Before you buy, ask:

- Does it cover pre-existing conditions?
- Is there a medical evacuation clause?
- How long can each trip be? (Some limit you to 30-60 days.)
- Are there age-related limitations?
- Do they offer direct billing, or is it reimbursement only?

Also, keep in mind that premiums often go up after age 65, and again at 70 and 75. The earlier you purchase and lock in coverage, the better.

If you travel often, investigate multi-trip annual insurance policies, which can be more cost-effective.

11. Tech Tools for Senior Travelers

Technology can be your best friend abroad. Learn how to use tools, such as:

- Google Maps for navigation

- WhatsApp or Skype for free international calls
- Translation apps for real-time language support
- Medication reminder apps to stay on schedule

Also, invest in an unlocked phone and local SIM card or a global roaming plan. This ensures you're reachable and can access help if needed.

Don't let fear of technology limit your experience, learn the basics before you go. Many libraries and community centres offer workshops on digital literacy for seniors.

12. Planning for Emergencies

Before you board a plane, cruise, or train, make sure you've prepared for the unexpected:

- Leave copies of your travel documents, itinerary, and insurance info with someone you trust.
- Wear a medical ID bracelet if you have major conditions.
- Know your country's embassy or consulate locations.
- Carry a basic first aid kit with essentials.

Most importantly, set up a communication plan with family or friends. Check in regularly, especially when changing locations or modes of transport.

Final Thoughts

Retirement doesn't mean your adventures have to stop, it means you now get to do them on your terms. But with age comes the responsibility to plan smarter. Travel can still be joyful, spontaneous, and life-changing, but the more you prepare, the more you'll enjoy.

Ask yourself:

- Do I understand my insurance?
- Have I planned for my health?
- Can I adapt to new environments?
- Am I willing to ask for help or slow down if needed?

With clear expectations, reliable resources, and the courage to adapt, travel in retirement can be one of the greatest joys of your life.

Just remember, travel isn't about ticking places off a list. It's about finding new parts of yourself, at any age, in places you never imagined.

So go ahead. Book the trip. Pack smart. And travel wisely.

Your adventure is still just beginning.

The Floating Retirement Dream

Imagine waking up to the sound of waves gently lapping against the hull, the scent of salt in the air, and the sunrise spilling across an endless ocean. For a growing number of retirees, this isn't just a vacation fantasy, it's everyday life. Living on a cruise ship has emerged as an unconventional but increasingly popular retirement option, promising luxury, adventure, and simplicity on the high seas.

But is it as dreamy as it sounds? What are the perks, pitfalls, and practicalities of making a cruise ship your permanent address? In this chapter, we dive into the full experience, the wonders and the challenges, of living aboard a floating city.

1. The Appeal of Cruise Ship Living

The idea of retiring on a cruise ship gained traction in the early 2000s when stories of savvy seniors comparing cruise costs to retirement homes began making headlines. And for good reason: cruises offer food, housekeeping, entertainment, medical support, and social interaction, often for a price comparable to (or even cheaper than) assisted living facilities in many countries.

Convenience and Comfort

Cruise ships are designed for ease. For retirees, this can be a game-changer. Elevators are plentiful, hallways are wide and smooth, and there's always someone available to assist with bags or mobility needs. Housekeeping takes care of your room, and dining staff remember your name (and dietary preferences). There's no lawn to mow, no groceries to shop for, and no car to maintain.

Endless Entertainment

From Broadway-style shows to trivia nights, yoga classes, art auctions, and lectures, cruise ships are buzzing with activities. Unlike traditional retirement homes, cruise living provides constant stimulation, new faces, and ever-changing views.

A Global Lifestyle

Perhaps the most appealing aspect is the ability to travel without the stress of packing, unpacking, or airport security. Your "home" travels with you. One week, you're watching glaciers in Alaska; the next, you're sipping espresso in Rome.

2. The Economics of Cruise Living

Living on a cruise ship full-time isn't cheap, but it can be surprisingly cost-effective when you tally up what's included.

Cost Comparison

The average monthly cost of a mid-range cruise is between $3,000 and $5,000 per person. That includes:

- Accommodation
- Meals (and snacks)
- Entertainment
- Housekeeping

- Transportation (to new places)
- Some level of medical care

Compare that to the average cost of an assisted living facility in the U.S., which hovers around $4,500 per month (excluding travel or extras), and the numbers start to align.

Frequent cruisers can leverage loyalty programs for discounts, and long-term stays may qualify for special pricing. Some lines even offer "world cruises" that last several months and provide reduced rates for extended guests.

3. The Challenges Below Deck

Cruise ship living isn't all umbrella drinks and ocean breezes. There are hurdles, and it's crucial to consider them.

Space Limitations

Cabins are compact. Storage is minimal, and living in a small room (with or without a window) can feel claustrophobic over time. Adjusting to the "tiny home" lifestyle requires mindset shifts and smart packing.

Health Considerations

While cruise ships have medical centres onboard, they're not hospitals. Serious health issues may require emergency evacuation, which can be costly and stressful. Add to this the cost of extensive insurance coverage. Additionally, long-term exposure to different climates, time zones, and cuisines can challenge your immune system.

Internet and Communication

Internet on ships can be slow, expensive, or unreliable, depending on the cruise line. Keeping in touch with family and friends can be difficult if you're constantly at sea. Some retirees invest in international phone plans or portable satellite internet devices.

Bureaucracy and Residency

Living on a cruise ship long-term raises the logistical questions:

- Where is your legal residence?
- How do you receive mail or prescriptions?
- What about taxes?

Some retirees maintain a home address through family or services like mail forwarding. It's important to speak with a financial advisor to understand implications for health coverage, pensions, and taxation.

4. The Emotional Landscape

Retiring on a cruise ship isn't just a logistical or financial choice, it's a profound lifestyle decision.

Constant Change

Some retirees love the thrill of new ports and changing scenery. For others, it can be disorienting or exhausting. Establishing routines can help maintain a sense of stability amid the motion.

Community Onboard

One of the great surprises for many cruise retirees is the vibrant community. Crew members and fellow passengers can become like family. Repeat guests often reconnect with familiar faces, and social events help build bonds.

However, transient friendships can also feel fleeting. Saying goodbye weekly to new acquaintances may become emotionally taxing.

Identity and Purpose

Without a home base, some retirees struggle with feelings of rootlessness. Others revel in the freedom. Hobbies, volunteer roles onboard, or remote work (yes, some retirees freelance!) can help maintain a sense of identity.

5. Choosing the Right Ship

Not all cruise lines are created equal. Some are better suited for long-term living.

Considerations:

- **Passenger Demographic**: Some ships cater to young partygoers; others attract retirees.
- **Onboard Amenities**: Look for ships with libraries, quiet lounges, enrichment classes, and wellness programs.
- **Medical Services**: Larger ships often have better-equipped medical centres.
- **Loyalty Programs**: Frequent travellers benefit from perks like priority boarding, room upgrades, and free laundry.

Lines like Holland America, Cunard, Princess, and Viking Ocean Cruises are often favoured by retirees for their refined atmospheres and age-appropriate entertainment.

6. A Day in the Life at Sea

Picture this: You wake to gentle movement and sunlight through your balcony doors. After breakfast in the dining room (eggs Benedict and fresh fruit), you join a tai chi class on the deck.

Mid-morning brings a lecture on Mediterranean history. After lunch, you stroll through the onboard art gallery or sit with a book in the library. Dinner is formal tonight, steak, wine, and candlelight, followed by a show in the theatre.

Or maybe you spend the day in port: exploring cathedrals in Spain, hiking volcanoes in Hawaii, or lounging on a Caribbean beach. Every day offers choices.

The key is that your days are structured but flexible. For many retirees, that balance is bliss.

7. Alternatives to Full-Time Ship Life

Not ready to give up land completely? Consider these hybrid options:

Back-to-Back Cruises

Book consecutive cruises on the same ship or cruise line. This gives you variety without constantly rebooking.

Seasonal Cruising

Spend winters on the water and summers at home. It's the snowbird lifestyle with a nautical twist.

Residential Ships

Some companies, like The World or the upcoming MV Narrative by Storylines, offer luxury residences at sea. These are floating condos with ownership options and curated global itineraries, but they come with hefty price tags.

8. The Psychology of Simplicity

Living on a cruise ship strips life to essentials: one suitcase, one room, one horizon. For many, this simplicity is deeply liberating.

- No clutter
- No errands
- No stress about home maintenance

Instead, your energy goes toward experience, connection, and personal growth. The sea has a way of encouraging reflection and presence.

Final Thoughts

Cruise ship living isn't for everyone. It requires flexibility, a sense of adventure, and a willingness to trade permanence for possibility.

Ask yourself:

- Do I thrive in social environments?
- Can I manage with limited space and shifting routines?
- Am I ready to prioritise experiences over possessions?

For those who say yes, the rewards are extraordinary. It's not just about seeing the world. It's about reimagining what retirement can be.

The ocean doesn't just carry you from place to place. It invites you to let go of old anchors and chart a course toward something entirely new. For some retirees, that's exactly the freedom they've been seeking.

So maybe the question isn't *why* live on a cruise ship. Maybe it's "why not?"

Retiring Abroad

Retirement no longer means settling down in the same town where you raised your family or even in the same country where you worked your entire life. In today's globalised world, retiring abroad is more accessible, affordable, and exciting than ever before. Many retirees are finding that they can enjoy a higher quality of life for a fraction of the cost by relocating overseas.

In this chapter, we'll explore how to retire abroad successfully, from the financial and legal logistics to selecting the best countries based on cost and safety. We'll also cover the benefits and challenges of making such a life-altering move.

Why Retire Abroad?

There are several reasons people consider retiring outside their home country:

- Lower cost of living
- Affordable healthcare
- Warmer climates
- Adventure and cultural enrichment
- Tax advantages in some jurisdictions

However, making this leap requires thoughtful planning and honest self-assessment. Are you comfortable being far from family? Are you adaptable to a different culture and language? Are you willing to navigate a foreign healthcare system?

If the answer is yes to these, retiring abroad could dramatically improve your financial and personal wellbeing.

Benefits of Retiring Abroad

1. **Financial Relief**
The most obvious benefit is cost. In many desirable countries, you can live comfortably on less than $2,000 per month, including rent, healthcare, and entertainment. Stretching your retirement dollars means a better lifestyle, more dining out, and extra travel.

2. **Improved Healthcare Access**
Many retirees find better and faster access to healthcare abroad. Countries like Thailand, Portugal, and Costa Rica offer world-class private healthcare at a fraction of U.S. prices. In some cases, you can walk into a clinic without an appointment and be seen within minutes.

3. **Enhanced Lifestyle and Climate**
Imagine trading winter snow for tropical breezes or dreary skies for sunny beaches. Retirees often move abroad to enjoy more consistent weather, beautiful scenery, and outdoor activities year-round.

4. **Cultural Enrichment**
Living abroad means experiencing new traditions, languages, foods, and perspectives. Many find this

cultural engagement invigorating, especially during retirement when time and freedom are abundant.

5. Expanding Social Circles
Expat communities are thriving in many parts of the world. You'll meet fellow retirees who have made the same move, making it easier to build new friendships and feel at home.

Key Financial Considerations

Before picking a country, it's essential to understand how your finances will translate overseas.

1. Cost of Living
In many countries, you can live comfortably on $1,500–$2,500 per month, including rent, utilities, healthcare, and food. Compare that to $4,000–$6,000 or more in many parts of the U.S., Canada, or Western Europe.

2. Housing
Rental costs vary dramatically. In Latin America or Southeast Asia, a modern 2-bedroom apartment in a safe neighbourhood might cost $400–$800/month. In contrast, that same apartment could run $2,000–$3,000 in the U.S. or Canada.

3. Healthcare
Many countries offer excellent private healthcare at a fraction of the cost in your home country. In places like Portugal or Thailand, you can get a doctor's visit

for $25 and a major surgery for a few thousand dollars. Some retirees opt for international health insurance, while others pay out-of-pocket due to affordability.

4. Taxes

Taxes are country specific. Some countries have no foreign income tax or generous exemptions for pensioners. Always consult a cross-border tax expert to avoid double taxation.

5. Currency Exchange and Banking

You'll need to account for currency fluctuations. Keep home country-based account for receiving Social Security or pension income and open a local bank account for daily expenses.

Legal and Practical Considerations

Residency and Visas

You can't just move to a country and stay indefinitely. You'll need to apply for a **r**etirement visa or long-term residence permit if you do not already have residency permits in that country. Each country has its own requirements. Most require:

- Proof of income (e.g., $1,000–$2,500/month depending on the country)
- Clean criminal record
- Proof of medical insurance

Healthcare Enrolment

In some countries, you can join the national healthcare system. Others require you to purchase private insurance. Always research coverage quality and enrolment timelines.

Language and Culture

Learning the basics of the local language will go a long way. Many expat-friendly countries have English-speaking communities, but adapting to the local culture is key for a fulfilling experience.

Cheapest and Safest Places to Retire Abroad (2025/26 Edition)

Here are some of the best retirement havens combining affordability, safety, healthcare, and expat friendliness:

1. Portugal

- **Monthly cost of living**: $2,000 – $2,500 (couple)
- **Safety**: One of the safest countries in Europe
- **Healthcare**: Excellent public and private systems
- **Residency**: D7 Visa available for retirees with stable passive income
- **Bonus**: Stunning coastline, rich culture, English widely spoken

2. Costa Rica

- **Monthly cost of living**: $1,800 – $2,200 (couple)
- **Safety**: High, especially in expat communities
- **Healthcare**: Strong private sector, public option via the CAJA system

- **Residency**: Pensionado visa requires $1,000/month in income
- **Bonus**: Lush landscapes, no military, eco-conscious nation

3. Mexico

- **Monthly cost of living**: $1,500 – $2,000 (couple)
- **Safety**: Varies by region (San Miguel de Allende, Lake Chapala are safe and popular)
- **Healthcare**: Modern private hospitals at low cost
- **Residency**: Temporary and permanent residency programs are accessible
- **Bonus**: Vibrant culture, low taxes

4. Malaysia

- **Monthly cost of living**: $1,300 – $1,800 (couple)
- **Safety**: Very safe, especially in Penang and Kuala Lumpur
- **Healthcare**: World-class private hospitals
- **Residency**: Malaysia My Second Home (MM2H) program
- **Bonus**: English is widely spoken, diverse cuisine, tropical weather

5. Ecuador

- **Monthly cost of living**: $1,200 – $1,800 (couple)
- **Safety**: Generally safe in expat-friendly areas like Cuenca

- **Healthcare**: Good urban medical care, affordable insurance
- **Residency**: Retirement visa with $1,275/month income requirement
- **Bonus**: U.S. dollar is the currency, mild climate in highlands

6. Thailand

- **Monthly cost of living**: $1,400 – $2,000 (couple)
- **Safety**: Safe and peaceful in expat zones
- **Healthcare**: Excellent hospitals and medical tourism reputation
- **Residency**: Retirement visa available at age 50+
- **Bonus**: Incredible cuisine, Buddhist culture, friendly locals

Hidden Gems to Watch

- **Bulgaria** (very affordable in the EU)
- **Nicaragua** (emerging expat destination)
- **Vietnam** (low cost and growing infrastructure)

Challenges of Retiring Abroad

While the benefits are substantial, retiring abroad isn't without its hurdles. It's important to consider these before making the leap:

1. Homesickness and Distance from Family

Being far from children, grandchildren, and lifelong friends can be difficult. Time zone differences and long travel distances may make regular visits rare.

2. Language Barriers

Even in expat-friendly places, speaking the local language is essential for integration and safety. Medical emergencies, legal issues, or even simple errands can become stressful if you can't communicate effectively.

3. Cultural Differences

From bureaucracy to business hours, every country operates differently. Patience and adaptability are key. You might be used to efficiency, but many places have a slower pace that requires adjustment.

Our Story – Prior to Retirement

We relocated from the United Kingdom to Canada after a great deal of thought and discussion. It wasn't a decision made lightly. We knew we wanted a fresh start, something new, something different, but also something that would still feel somewhat familiar. We explored several possibilities: New Zealand, Australia, the United States. All English-speaking countries. That wasn't a coincidence. At our age, learning a new language fluently felt like more stress than adventure, and we wanted the challenge to be joyful, not frustrating.

After months of research, conversations, and sleepless nights weighing pros and cons, we chose the West Coast of Canada. The pull of mountains, forests, and ocean was hard to resist, and the

> lifestyle felt aligned with what we were looking for, balanced, peaceful, but still full of opportunity.
>
> That said, the transition wasn't seamless. One of the first hurdles we faced was discovering that our UK qualifications didn't translate well here. We had to reestablish our footing professionally and financially. And let's not even begin to talk about the housing prices, it was quite a shock. But adaptation, we've learned, is a muscle that only gets stronger with use. Over time, we found our rhythm and began to feel more rooted.
>
> There are still moments that remind us we're not from here, mainly, the constant comments about our accents. Canadians seem genuinely delighted by them. If our biggest challenge now is being asked to repeat ourselves with a smile, we'll happily take it. It's been a journey worth every step.

4. Healthcare Limitations

While healthcare can be excellent in many countries, there are limitations. Rural areas might not have advanced facilities. You may also need to travel for specialist care or certain medications.

5. Legal and Financial Complexity

Managing cross-border taxes, property ownership, and currency exchange can be complex. It's essential to work with professionals who specialise in international retirement planning.

6. Political and Economic Stability

Always assess a country's long-term stability. An economic downturn or political shift can impact residency status, inflation, or safety.

Is Retiring Abroad Right for You?

Retiring abroad isn't for everyone. It requires flexibility, patience, and openness to new experiences. But for those who are ready, it can mean more than just saving money, it's about adding years of adventure, comfort, and vitality to your life.

Before making the move:

- **Visit first** – spend several months in your chosen country.
- **Talk to expats** – join forums and Facebook groups.
- **Work with experts** – visa agents, tax advisors, and real estate pros.

Retirement doesn't mean slowing down, it can be a bold new chapter. And the world is ready to welcome you.

Flexible Work / Entrepreneurship

Retirement has traditionally been viewed as a time to step away from the workforce and embrace rest, travel, and leisurely activities. However, the modern retiree is reshaping this narrative. Today, many individuals entering retirement are seeking opportunities for flexible work or entrepreneurial ventures. These endeavours not only offer supplemental income but also provide purpose, mental stimulation, and social engagement. In this chapter, we explore the growing trend of flexible work and entrepreneurship among retirees, including the benefits, challenges, and practical steps for getting started.

The Evolution of Retirement

The concept of retirement has undergone a significant transformation over the past few decades. Historically, retirement was a definitive end to one's career, marked by a pension and a withdrawal from economic activity. Today, with increased life expectancy, better health in later years, and shifts in financial planning, many retirees are opting to remain professionally active in various capacities.

The desire to stay engaged, contribute to society, and maintain a sense of identity and purpose drives many to seek flexible or entrepreneurial work. For others, the motivation may be financial, either to supplement retirement savings or to support a desired lifestyle.

Benefits of Working in Retirement

1. **Financial Security** Working during retirement can ease financial pressure. Many retirees find that their pensions or savings are insufficient to cover the cost of living, especially with rising healthcare costs. Flexible work or business income can fill this gap.
2. **Mental and Emotional Well-being** Staying professionally active helps maintain cognitive function and emotional health. Work offers structure, routine, and a sense of accomplishment, which can be particularly beneficial after leaving a long-term career.
3. **Social Interaction** Retirement can sometimes lead to social isolation. Working or starting a business can provide valuable opportunities to interact with others, build networks, and form new relationships.
4. **Personal Fulfilment** For many, retirement is the perfect time to pursue long-held passions or explore new interests. Starting a business or consulting in a field of expertise can be immensely rewarding.

Types of Flexible Work Opportunities

Flexible work encompasses a variety of arrangements that allow retirees to earn income without committing to a traditional full-time job. Some of the most popular options include:

1. **Part-Time Employment** Many retirees choose part-time jobs that offer lower stress and flexible hours. These might include roles in retail, customer service, education, or healthcare. Part-time work provides steady income and keeps retirees connected to the workforce.

2. Freelancing and Consulting Retirees with specialised skills and experience often find freelancing or consulting to be a lucrative and flexible option. Whether it's writing, graphic design, business consulting, or IT support, freelancing allows individuals to work on their own terms.

3. Gig Economy Jobs Platforms like Uber, TaskRabbit, or Airbnb enable retirees to earn income through short-term or one-time jobs. This work can be ideal for those seeking maximum flexibility and variety.

4. Seasonal Work Certain industries, such as tourism, retail, and agriculture, offer seasonal jobs that align well with retirees' availability. These roles can also provide unique experiences, such as working at national parks or holiday resorts.

5. Remote and Online Jobs Technology has opened the door to remote work in fields like customer support, transcription, tutoring, and virtual assistance. These jobs allow retirees to work from home and set their own schedules.

Entrepreneurship in Retirement

Starting a business in retirement is an exciting and increasingly common path. With a wealth of experience, networks, and often a clearer sense of purpose, retirees are well-positioned to succeed as entrepreneurs.

1. Identifying a Business Idea

Successful retirement businesses often stem from personal interests, hobbies, or professional expertise. Common business ideas include:

- Consulting or coaching

- Craft or art sales
- Pet services
- Tutoring or education services
- Online stores or e-commerce
- Blogging or content creation

2. Creating a Business Plan

A clear business plan is essential for success. It should outline the business goals, target market, pricing strategy, marketing approach, and financial projections. Many local small business centres and online platforms offer free resources and templates to help.

3. Funding the Business

Retirees may choose to self-fund their businesses using savings, but other options include small business loans, grants, or investments from family and friends. It's important to assess the financial risks and ensure that starting a business won't compromise long-term retirement security.

Our Story – Working in Retirement

As part of our retirement planning, we explored the many ways we could stay active, engaged, and generate a little income. We weren't ready to spend our days on the sofa watching daytime television or filling time with idle distractions. We wanted our retirement to be purposeful, but still on our own terms. So, we began looking into options for part-time work, volunteer roles, and even franchise opportunities.

To our surprise, the possibilities were plentiful. From local shops to community programs, there seemed to be no shortage of opportunities for retirees who wanted to keep busy. After a few months of weighing the options, my wife had a wonderful idea, one that combined enjoyment, culture, and a bit of entrepreneurial spirit. We opened a small shop in our new hometown, selling items from our homeland: traditional food, ornaments, and keepsakes that brought a bit of the UK to our Canadian neighbours.

This shop has become more than just a business; it's a social hub. One of us is there every day, chatting with locals, meeting travellers, and sharing stories with curious passersby. It's given us a new sense of connection and purpose without the stress of the corporate world we left behind.

We've decided that this is enough. Between the shop, our hobbies, and our ongoing travel plans, we've managed to build a life that feels full and entirely ours. We answer to only ourselves, and that's the beauty of retirement done right. No bosses, no deadlines, just days filled with meaning, variety, and joy.

4. Marketing and Growth

Marketing is crucial for any new business. Retirees should leverage social media, networking groups, and local events to promote their offerings. Word-of-mouth referrals and excellent customer service can also drive growth.

Challenges and Considerations

While the rewards of flexible work and entrepreneurship can be significant, retirees should be mindful of the potential challenges:

1. **Physical and Cognitive Demands** Work, especially if it involves physical labour or complex tasks, can be

taxing. It's important to choose roles or business models that align with current capabilities.

2. Time Management Balancing work with other retirement goals, such as travel or family time, can be tricky. Retirees should clearly define their availability and boundaries to maintain a healthy work-life balance.

3. Technology Gaps Many flexible work and entrepreneurial opportunities require digital skills. While this can be a barrier, numerous community centres and online platforms offer training and support for older adults.

4. Financial Implications Earnings from work or a business may affect taxes, Social Security benefits, or healthcare eligibility. Consulting with a financial advisor is recommended to understand the full impact.

5. Legal and Regulatory Issues Entrepreneurs must consider licensing, zoning, business structure, and liability. Understanding local regulations and obtaining proper insurance is crucial.

Steps to Get Started

1. Self-Assessment Begin by evaluating your interests, strengths, and motivations. What activities energise you? What skills do you enjoy using? This self-awareness will guide you to the most fulfilling opportunities.

2. Explore Opportunities Research potential roles, industries, or business ideas. Talk to others who are working in retirement, attend workshops, and use online platforms like LinkedIn, Upwork, or SCORE.

3. Update Your Skills, If necessary, take courses to refresh or develop new skills. Many free or low-cost options are available through community colleges, libraries, and online sites like Coursera or Udemy.
4. Create a Plan Whether you're seeking a job or starting a business, a plan will help clarify your goals, strategy, and steps to take. Set realistic expectations and milestones.
5. Start Small Ease into your new venture to test the waters. For example, take on a few freelance gigs or start selling a few products online before committing more time or resources.
6. Monitor and Adjust Regularly review your progress and adjust as needed. Flexibility is key, and your interests or circumstances may change over time.

Real-Life Stories

John, 68 – Freelance Accountant After retiring from a 40-year career in accounting, John wanted to stay active without the stress of full-time work. He began offering tax preparation services from home during the busy season. This not only supplemented his income but also kept him engaged with clients and peers.

Linda, 62 – Etsy Shop Owner Linda turned her lifelong passion for knitting into a small business. She opened an Etsy store to sell handmade scarves and sweaters. The business grew through social media and craft fairs, bringing in steady income and personal satisfaction.

Carlos, 70 – Tour Guide Carlos loved history and lived in a city full of historical landmarks. He launched a guided walking tour business tailored to senior travellers.

His knowledge and warm personality made his tours a hit, and he now runs them part-time during the tourist season.

Conclusion

Flexible work and entrepreneurship in retirement offer a powerful combination of financial, mental, and emotional benefits. Whether driven by necessity or a desire for fulfilment, retirees today have more opportunities than ever to remain active and impactful. With thoughtful planning, a willingness to learn, and the courage to explore new paths, retirement can be the beginning of a dynamic and rewarding new chapter.

Time and Energy in Retirement

Retirement is often envisioned as the ultimate freedom: a blank slate of time to pursue leisure, hobbies, travel, and rest. Yet, many retirees find themselves overwhelmed, scattered, or even under-stimulated. Without the structure of a traditional work schedule, managing time and energy becomes both a challenge and an opportunity. In this chapter, we explore how to effectively balance flexible work, leisure activities, and personal priorities to create a fulfilling and harmonious retirement lifestyle.

The Paradox of Free Time

One of the great ironies of retirement is that having too much time can lead to dissatisfaction if it lacks direction. The abrupt transition from a full-time career to unstructured days can feel disorienting. Without intentional planning, retirees may struggle with procrastination, low motivation, or a sense of purposelessness.

Time management in retirement isn't about cramming every hour with activity; rather, it's about aligning your time with what matters most to you. This includes your values, health, interests, relationships, and long-term goals.

Understanding Energy Rhythms

Effective time management also requires understanding your personal energy cycles. Unlike during a career, when schedules are often dictated by employers, retirees can now align their tasks with their natural rhythms.

Morning People vs. Night Owls: Know when you are most alert and energetic. If mornings are your peak, schedule focused or demanding tasks then. Save lighter activities for low-energy periods.

Physical and Mental Demands: Consider both the physical and cognitive load of activities. For example, yard work and exercise may drain physical energy, while writing or planning might be mentally taxing.

Recharge Strategies: Include regular breaks, rest, and recovery in your day. Short naps, walks, meditation, or quiet reading can restore energy and prevent burnout.

The Pillars of Time and Energy Balance

Creating a balanced retirement involves intentionally distributing your time and energy across several key areas:

Purposeful Work: This might be part-time employment, volunteering, or entrepreneurship. It should bring a sense of purpose without dominating your time.

Personal Health: Physical activity, nutrition, sleep, and medical care form the foundation of sustainable energy. Prioritise your health as the enabler of everything else.

Leisure and Hobbies: Retirement is the perfect time to dive into hobbies, learn new skills, or simply enjoy unstructured play and exploration.

Relationships and Community: Maintaining strong social connections with family, friends, and neighbours supports emotional well-being and prevents isolation.

Rest and Reflection: Build in quiet time for reading, meditation, journaling, or simply being. This fosters mental clarity and emotional resilience.

Creating a Personal Schedule

Even if your days are unstructured, having a loose routine can help you stay grounded and intentional. Here's how to build a retirement schedule that serves your lifestyle:

Step 1: Define Your Priorities Start by listing what matters most. For example:

- Staying healthy and active
- Spending time with grandchildren
- Traveling a few times a year
- Growing a home-based business
- Learning a new language

Step 2: Audit Your Time Track how you currently spend your days for a week. Use a simple journal or app to note when you wake up, eat, relax, work, socialise, or engage in hobbies.

Step 3: Identify Time Leaks Are there hours lost to aimless scrolling, excessive TV, or procrastination? Becoming aware of time leaks helps you make more conscious choices.

Step 4: Design Your Ideal Week Using your priorities and energy patterns, map out a flexible weekly schedule. Include blocks for different types of activities:

- Mornings for focused work or exercise
- Afternoons for socialising, errands, or hobbies
- Evenings for relaxation or entertainment

Step 5: Build in Flexibility Leave buffer time between activities. Retirement should feel spacious, not rigid. Allow room for spontaneity and rest.

Tools and Techniques for Time Management

Several tools and strategies can enhance your ability to stay organised and energised:

Time Blocking Allocate specific blocks of time for categories of tasks. This helps prevent overcommitting and creates structure without a strict hourly schedule.

The "Three Big Things" Rule Each day, identify the three most important things you want to accomplish. This keeps your day focused and rewarding.

Digital Tools Use calendars, reminder apps, or task managers like Google Calendar, Todoist, or Trello to stay organised.

Weekly Reviews Take time each weekend to reflect on the past week. What went well? What felt off? Adjust your upcoming week accordingly.

Managing Energy, Not Just Time

Time is finite, but energy can be replenished. Managing energy effectively is crucial to sustaining a joyful retirement.

Sleep Hygiene Stick to a consistent sleep schedule. Avoid screens before bed, create a restful sleep environment, and aim for 7-9 hours of sleep.

Physical Activity Regular movement boosts energy and mood. Find activities you enjoy – walking, swimming, dancing, yoga – and integrate them into your daily routine.

Nutrition Eat balanced meals with a focus on whole foods. Stay hydrated and limit sugar, alcohol, and processed foods that sap energy.

Mental Engagement Stimulate your brain with puzzles, reading, creative arts, or learning new skills. Mental engagement preserves cognitive health and prevents boredom.

Emotional Self-Care Practice gratitude, mindfulness, and emotional awareness. Stay connected with positive influences and seek support when needed.

Avoiding Common Time Traps

Even in retirement, it's easy to fall into habits that drain time and energy:

Overcommitment You may feel obligated to say yes to every volunteer request or social invite. Learn to decline graciously when your schedule is full.

Lack of Boundaries Working from home or running a business can blur the line between personal and work time. Set clear work hours and unplug regularly.

Perfectionism Retirement is not about productivity perfection. Allow yourself to pursue activities for joy, not just outcomes.

Isolation While rest is important, too much alone time can be draining. Make regular plans to connect with others.

Unrealistic Expectations You don't need to master five hobbies, remodel your home, and volunteer three days a week. Pace yourself.

Our Story – Time Management

If you've followed our journey through this book, you'll know that our days are anything but idle. Between running a shop, travelling, pursuing hobbies, and keeping our social lives active, we manage to pack in quite a bit. Yet somehow, we still find time to enjoy a quiet coffee on the porch, share a glass of wine in the evening, tend to our garden, and most importantly, spend time with our children. The secret? Time management, not the rigid, corporate kind, but a more personal, flexible version that suits our retired life.

In the beginning, we struggled. Some days felt overwhelmingly busy, while others felt aimless. We were either doing too much or wondering what to do next. It was an odd adjustment after years of structured work life. Eventually, we began to create a simple system, not a strict schedule, but a thoughtful approach to our time. We listed the things we needed and wanted to do, then slowly shaped a rhythm around them.

Now, we operate with a comfortable balance. Our days feel full but not rushed. The shop opens when we want it to. Our travel is paced. Our garden flourishes under careful attention, and we've carved out quiet spaces in the day to read, reflect, or simply rest.

Time management, we've come to learn, isn't about cramming the calendar. It's about prioritising joy. It's choosing what matters and giving those things your time, rather than letting time slip away. Retirement isn't the end of routine, it's the chance to build a better one.

Real-Life Rhythm Examples

Marcia, 66 – Balanced Entrepreneur Marcia runs a small online craft store. She works three mornings a week, reserving afternoons for walks, reading, and time with her grandkids. Her weekends are tech-free, devoted to nature and relaxation.

Glenn, 71 – Volunteer with Structure Glenn volunteers two days a week at a local shelter and spends three days on creative writing. He schedules regular lunch dates with friends and guards his evenings for quiet time with his partner.

Priya, 63 – Curious Explorer Priya spends her mornings on a language learning app and yoga. Afternoons vary: sometimes she travels, other times she teaches online cooking classes. She blocks Fridays as "open space" for anything spontaneous.

The Joy of a Well-Balanced Retirement

Ultimately, a fulfilling retirement is less about how much you do and more about how aligned your activities are with your personal values and energy. The goal isn't to stay busy, it's to stay meaningful, healthy, and engaged.

Time and energy are precious currencies. With intentional planning, clear boundaries, and space for rest and renewal, you can design a retirement lifestyle that is not only productive but also deeply satisfying.

In the next chapter, we will explore how to build and maintain strong social connections that enrich your retirement years and support long-term mental and emotional well-being.

Building Meaningful Connections

Retirement often brings a significant shift in social dynamics. While the daily interactions with colleagues and the structure of the workplace fade away, the need for connection remains vital. In fact, strong social ties are one of the most important predictors of long-term happiness, health, and even longevity in retirement. In this chapter, we'll explore how to intentionally cultivate, nurture, and enjoy meaningful relationships during your retirement years.

The Importance of Social Connection

Human beings are inherently social creatures. Studies have shown that social isolation and loneliness can increase the risk of depression, cognitive decline, heart disease, and even mortality. On the flip side, retirees who maintain rich social networks report higher life satisfaction, better physical health, and a greater sense of purpose.

Social connection not only fills time; it fills the soul. A conversation with a friend, a shared laugh, or a helping hand all serve to remind us that we belong, that we matter, and that we are still deeply embedded in a web of human interaction. As one retires, this truth becomes even more evident, relationships are not just enjoyable, they are essential.

Types of Social Connections

It's important to recognise that social connection comes in many forms. A well-balanced social life includes a mix of different relationships:

1. Family Bonds: Children, grandchildren, siblings, and extended family can provide emotional support, shared memories, and a sense of belonging. Intergenerational relationships, in particular, are rewarding. Grandparents often find renewed purpose and energy when involved in their grandchildren's lives, whether through babysitting, storytelling, or attending school events.

2. Friendships: Lifelong friends and new ones alike offer companionship, laughter, and shared experiences. These are the people you can call in a moment of joy or distress. Making time to nourish these bonds, through coffee dates, hobby-sharing, or just regular calls, helps you stay grounded.

3. Community Ties: Neighbours, club members, faith groups, or civic organisations can help retirees feel integrated and active in their community. They create a sense of place and purpose, offering both social opportunities and the joy of giving back.

4. Interest-Based Groups: Whether it's a book club, hiking group, gardening club, or bridge night, shared interests foster deep connections. These activities also keep your mind sharp and your schedule exciting.

5. Digital Networks: Online communities can be a valuable supplement, especially for those with mobility challenges or who live in rural areas. Engaging in online forums, attending virtual classes, or simply using social media can enhance connectivity.

Transitioning from Work-Based Relationships

Leaving the workforce often means losing a built-in social structure. To maintain or replace these connections:

- Stay in touch with former coworkers through regular catch-ups, alumni groups, or social media. Schedule a monthly lunch or coffee with a group of former colleagues.
- Attend reunions or industry events, if desired. These provide excellent networking opportunities and help you stay intellectually engaged.
- Reconnect with friends you've lost touch with over the years. Retirement can be the perfect time to revive old friendships that got lost in the busyness of life.
- Join local groups or volunteer opportunities that align with your skills and values. This not only reestablishes routine but also broadens your social horizons.

Creating New Social Opportunities

Retirement offers the freedom to meet new people and forge fresh connections:

1. Volunteerism: Giving your time to causes you care about not only helps others but also connects you with like-minded people. Whether you're tutoring kids, working at an animal shelter, or helping at a food bank, volunteering fosters both empathy and camaraderie.

2. Lifelong Learning: Enrol in classes at local colleges, community centres, or online platforms. Education stimulates your mind and introduces you to fellow learners. Try new subjects, art history, computer programming, or foreign languages can ignite new passions and friendships.

3. Clubs and Hobby Groups: Whether it's painting, biking, knitting, or astronomy, there's likely a group for it. If not, start one! Putting up flyers at local community centres or posting in online groups can quickly gather interest.

4. Travel Groups: Organised tours and cultural exchanges provide opportunities to connect with fellow explorers. These shared adventures create instant bonds and unforgettable memories.

5. Faith and Spiritual Groups: Religious or spiritual communities often provide a built-in support system and opportunities for regular gatherings. They also foster a sense of meaning and shared values.

6. Support and Wellness Groups: Retirement can bring unexpected challenges, from health concerns to caregiving responsibilities. Support groups create a space for empathy, encouragement, and shared resilience.

Strengthening Existing Relationships

Retirement is also a time to invest more deeply in the relationships you already have:

- Schedule regular family meals or game nights. Routine gatherings create structure and something to look forward to.
- Make weekly phone or video calls with long-distance loved ones. Consistency builds stronger emotional bonds.

- Plan trips or retreats with friends. Whether it's a weekend getaway or a cruise, shared adventures deepen relationships.
- Write letters or send postcards as a heartfelt way to stay connected. In an age of instant communication, a handwritten note carries emotional weight.
- Create collaborative traditions, such as group cooking, gardening projects, or book circles.

Overcoming Social Hurdles

Many retirees face challenges in building and maintaining social connections:

1. **Mobility or Health Issues:** Consider accessible events, virtual meetups, or transportation assistance through community services. Libraries, senior centres, and local councils often offer programs tailored for varying abilities.
2. **Introversion or Shyness:** Start with smaller, more intimate gatherings. Focus on one-on-one connections instead of large groups. Online interaction can also be a gentler entry point into social engagement.
3. **Loss and Grief:** If you've lost a spouse or close friends, allow yourself time to grieve. Support groups and counselling can be helpful. Creating new connections doesn't replace your loss but offers emotional sustenance.
4. **Relocation:** Moving to a new area can be disorienting. Look for welcome clubs, newcomers' groups, or community bulletin boards to ease the transition. Introduce yourself to neighbours and attend community events.

Digital Tools for Staying Connected

Technology can be a powerful ally in maintaining social ties:

- **Video Calls:** Use Zoom, FaceTime, or Skype for face-to-face conversations. Virtual dinner dates or game nights can bring loved ones together across distances.
- **Social Media:** Facebook, Instagram, and other platforms help you stay updated on friends and family. Use them to share updates, photos, and articles of interest.
- **Messaging Apps:** WhatsApp, Signal, or GroupMe allow for easy group chats and daily updates. You can stay part of the small, day-to-day moments.
- **Online Groups:** Forums and platforms like Meetup.com can introduce you to virtual communities based on shared interests. Try joining one or two groups and contributing regularly.

Technology might feel overwhelming at first, but many libraries and community centres offer free courses on digital literacy. Don't hesitate to ask a friend or grandchild for help setting up apps and devices.

The Role of Pets and Nature

Social connection isn't limited to humans. Pets can provide emotional support, routine, and unconditional companionship. Walking a dog often leads to spontaneous chats with neighbours. Pets also offer a comforting presence during quieter moments.

Additionally, engaging with nature, through community gardens, walking groups, or birdwatching, can foster shared experiences and introduce you to new people. Outdoor activities promote physical well-being and naturally create bonding opportunities.

Nature also offers a sense of peace and belonging. Shared outdoor experiences, picnics, hikes, sunrise yoga, can nurture both new and existing relationships.

Real-Life Social Strategies

Margaret, 70 – The Connector Margaret began hosting a monthly neighbourhood potluck after retiring. It started with five households and has grown into a tight-knit community that supports each other in times of need. Her gatherings now feature themes, guest speakers, and music.

Ron, 67 – The Volunteer Mentor After decades as an engineer, Ron now mentors' young students in STEM through a local nonprofit. He finds joy in their curiosity and energy, and the relationships have enriched his own learning. Ron also organises meetups for retired engineers to share stories and teach workshops.

Leila, 73 – The Digital Socialite Leila lives in a rural area but stays connected through multiple online book clubs and Facebook groups for gardeners. She uses video calls to catch up weekly with her children and grandchildren. Leila even started her own blog, sharing gardening tips and stories.

Building a Weekly Social Plan

Just as with time and energy management, building social connections can benefit from intentional planning. Here's how:

1. Identify Your Social Needs: Do you thrive on daily contact or prefer deeper, less frequent interactions? Know your preferences and energy levels.
2. List Key Relationships: Identify people you want to stay connected with regularly. Keep a contact list and rotate through your connections monthly.
3. Schedule Social Time: Block time each week for phone calls, meetups, or social activities. Even a 20-minute walk with a friend counts.
4. Try New Things: Step out of your comfort zone regularly by joining a new group or reaching out to someone new. Say yes to invitations more often.
5. Reflect and Adjust: At the end of the month, ask yourself: What social moments brought me joy? What felt like a chore? Adjust accordingly. Make it a goal to improve your social satisfaction each month.

Our Story – Staying Connected

One thing we haven't mentioned until now is our age, we're in our mid-sixties. Old enough, as the saying goes, to know better, but young enough in spirit to still seek out adventure and connection. When we moved countries, we left behind more than a familiar landscape, we left a lifetime of relationships, routines, and the day-to-day presence of our three grown children, who now live their own full, exciting lives.

But distance hasn't meant disconnection. We've found new ways to stay close, even across time zones. Video calls, shared photos, and the occasional message just to say "thinking of you" keep us emotionally grounded. Social media, used wisely, has become a powerful tool to feel close, even when we're far apart. It's not a replacement for physical presence, but it helps bridge the gap.

Locally, we've made strong new connections. Our friends here have come from many corners of life, some through shared hobbies, others through community events, and quite a few through our little shop. It's amazing what a simple conversation at the counter can lead to. We've shared stories, laughs, even recipes with people we never would've met otherwise. The shop has become more than a business, it's a social hub, a door to friendship.

Staying connected in retirement requires intention. It means making the effort to reach out, say yes to invitations, and seek out kindred spirits. We've also learned that it's equally important to distance ourselves from toxic relationships. Retirement is too precious to spend in the company of negativity.

Find your people. Nurture your relationships. Connection is the heartbeat of a fulfilling life, no matter where you live, or how old you are.

Social Connection and Emotional Health

Human connection isn't just about filling time; it's about emotional wellness. Regular social contact reduces stress, increases your sense of security, and helps guard against mental health challenges like depression and anxiety. When you laugh with others, share stories, or feel heard, your brain releases oxytocin, a hormone that promotes bonding and reduces stress.

Retirement often brings emotional shifts. Social networks serve as a buffer, helping you adjust to your new identity and routines. They remind you that you're still needed, loved, and relevant.

Conclusion

In retirement, meaningful social connection is not a luxury, it's a lifeline. Staying socially engaged protects your health, boosts your happiness, and adds richness to your days. With a blend of old friends and new encounters, structured gatherings and spontaneous chats, you can build a retirement that is not only active but also deeply connected.

Start where you are. Reach out. Join in. Make a call. Say yes. Every connection you make is a step toward a fuller, richer, and more joyful retirement.

Strong Social Connections

Retirement is a major life transition, bringing with it newfound freedom, time, and opportunity. However, with this freedom often comes a surprising challenge: loneliness. The social networks once maintained by daily work routines may dwindle or vanish. As a result, cultivating and preserving strong social connections becomes more than a lifestyle choice; it becomes essential to emotional health and longevity.

In this chapter, we delve into how to intentionally build and sustain meaningful relationships in retirement, ensuring your later years are rich in companionship, belonging, and support.

Why Social Connection Matters More Than Ever

Decades of research confirm what many intuitively feel, humans are social beings. In retirement, where structured social settings like the workplace dissolve, the quality of our relationships becomes even more critical. Studies from Harvard and the National Institute on Aging have shown that individuals with strong social ties enjoy better cognitive function, lower rates of depression, increased life satisfaction, and even longer lifespans.

Loneliness, on the other hand, can be as harmful as smoking 15 cigarettes a day. It weakens the immune system, raises stress hormones, and increases the risk of dementia and heart disease. In this context, building social ties is a form of preventive medicine.

Step 1: Assess Your Current Social Landscape

Before you can build, you must understand what's already in place. Ask yourself:

- Who do I connect with regularly?
- Which relationships energise me? Which drain me?
- How often do I engage socially each week?
- Are there areas in my life that feel socially empty, e.g., spiritual, recreational, intellectual?

Mapping your social connections can reveal gaps and opportunities. Some people have family but few close friends. Others have many acquaintances but few deep relationships. Self-awareness is the foundation for building a balanced social life.

Step 2: Strengthen Existing Relationships

Often, the most rewarding social connections are already within reach. Retirement offers the time and flexibility to deepen those bonds:

- **Schedule Weekly Check-Ins**: Make a standing coffee date, video call, or walk with a friend or family member.
- **Revive Old Friendships:** Reconnect with friends from college, past jobs, or old neighbourhoods. A simple message, "I was thinking of you and wondered how you're doing," can reopen the door.
- **Be Present:** Show up not just physically, but emotionally. Listen actively, ask thoughtful questions, and avoid multitasking during conversations.

Strong relationships are maintained with consistency and care. Even small efforts, birthday texts, shared articles, or mailed notes, signal that someone matters to you.

Step 3: Cultivate New Connections

Meeting new people as an older adult may feel daunting, but it's deeply rewarding. Here's how to get started:

- **Join Local Clubs:** Whether it's a gardening group, photography class, or book club, shared interests make socialising easier.
- **Volunteer:** Choose causes that align with your values. Volunteering not only fills time with purpose but introduces you to like-minded individuals.
- **Attend Community Events:** Look for senior centre activities, cultural festivals, lectures, and hobby expos. Show up regularly, and your face becomes familiar.
- **Use Technology:** Platforms like Meetup, Facebook Groups, and even Reddit can connect you with people nearby or around the world who share your passions.

Remember, friendship takes time. Be patient and open. Not every new connection will bloom into something deep, but some will.

Step 4: Foster Intergenerational Relationships

Social connections across age groups add vitality and perspective to retirement life:

- **Mentorship**: Share your skills with younger generations, through schools, nonprofits, or informal relationships.
- **Family Engagement**: Spend time with grandchildren, nieces, and nephews. Offer to babysit, help with homework, or attend their events.
- **Cross-Generational Clubs**: Many organisations intentionally mix ages to encourage dialogue and community.

These relationships can keep you feeling young and informed, while providing younger people with invaluable wisdom and support.

Step 5: Embrace Vulnerability and Openness

Making and keeping friends requires emotional courage. Especially as we age, it can be easy to fall into the trap of "people already have their circles." But relationships grow when we:

- Initiate conversations
- Offer help and ask for it
- Share our thoughts and feelings with authenticity
- Show appreciation and affection

Vulnerability builds trust. By being open, you invite others to do the same.

Step 6: Avoid Toxic Relationships

While connection is vital, not all relationships are beneficial. Retirement is a time to cultivate peace and positivity. Pay attention to people who:

- Consistently drain your energy
- Are critical or dismissive

- Make you feel unsafe or diminished

Give yourself permission to limit or end these relationships. Surround yourself with those who celebrate, support, and challenge you in healthy ways.

Step 7: Create Social Rituals and Traditions

Building structure into your social life adds rhythm and reliability:

- Weekly Potlucks or Game Nights
- Monthly Book Club or Film Discussion
- Annual Trips or Retreats with Friends
- Holiday Gatherings or Theme Dinners

Rituals don't have to be elaborate. Even small, predictable interactions help relationships thrive.

Step 8: Use Technology as a Bridge, Not a Barrier

Tech can both connect and isolate. Use it intentionally:

- **Video Calls**: FaceTime, Zoom, or Google Meet for long-distance friends.
- **Messaging Apps**: WhatsApp, GroupMe, or Signal for casual updates and group chats.
- **Social Media**: Facebook for family photos, Instagram for hobbies, and niche forums for specific interests.

Don't be afraid to learn. Ask for help from younger relatives or take a tech literacy class at your local library or senior centre.

Step 9: Integrate Social Activity with Physical Wellness

Exercise is more fun, and more likely to stick, when it's social:

- Join a walking group
- Attend yoga or tai chi classes
- Try group sports like pickleball, dancing, or swimming

These activities boost mood, encourage accountability, and offer social outlets.

Step 10: Recognise the Mental and Emotional Benefits

Strong social connections can:

- Reduce risk of depression and anxiety
- Improve cognitive function and memory
- Build resilience in times of stress or grief
- Enhance self-worth and belonging

Relationships act as emotional anchors. They remind us we are seen, valued, and loved.

Real Stories: Retirement Relationships in Action

Gloria, 74, Urban Explorer When Gloria retired, she joined a city walking tour group. She's now close friends with three other retirees, and they plan monthly adventures to new parts of town.

Ed and Maria, 68 and 71, The Dinner Hosts Every Sunday, Ed and Maria host "Soup Night." Friends bring bread, wine, or dessert, and conversations stretch into the evening. Over the years, it's become a cherished ritual.

Kofi, 69, The Mentor A retired architect, Kofi volunteers at a youth design club. His mentorship has led to friendships with both students and fellow volunteers.

Connection is a Practice

Strong social connections don't just happen, they are nurtured. Retirement grants you the time and autonomy to prioritise people and practices that bring you joy, meaning, and belonging. Start small. Reach out. Say yes. Follow up. Invest.

The rewards, a more joyful, resilient, and mentally vibrant retirement, are well worth the effort.

Staying Healthy in Your Senior Years

Aging is a natural and inevitable process, but how we age, both physically and mentally, can be greatly influenced by the lifestyle choices we make. As people move into their senior years, maintaining health becomes less about preventing aging itself and more about maximising quality of life, preserving independence, and fostering vitality. This chapter offers a comprehensive guide on how to stay healthy in your senior years by focusing on nutrition, physical activity, mental health, preventative care, and social engagement.

The Pillars of Healthy Aging

Staying healthy as you, age involves a multi-faceted approach. It includes physical well-being, emotional stability, mental sharpness, social connectedness, and a proactive approach to healthcare. By focusing on the key pillars of healthy aging, you can enhance your well-being and enjoy a fulfilling and active retirement.

1. Nutrition: Fuelling Your Body for Longevity

Proper nutrition is essential to maintaining strength, energy, and overall wellness in older adulthood. As the body ages, metabolism slows, and the need for certain nutrients increases while caloric needs may decrease.

A Balanced Diet

- **Fruits and Vegetables**: Aim for at least 5 servings per day. These provide essential vitamins, minerals, and antioxidants that help fight disease and boost immune function.
- **Whole Grains**: Choose whole grain bread, oatmeal, brown rice, and quinoa over refined grains. They help maintain healthy blood sugar levels and provide sustained energy.
- **Lean Proteins**: Incorporate sources like fish, poultry, eggs, beans, and legumes. Protein is essential for muscle maintenance and repair.
- **Healthy Fats**: Focus on unsaturated fats found in olive oil, nuts, avocados, and fatty fish. Limit saturated and trans fats.
- **Calcium and Vitamin D**: Important for bone health. Sources include dairy products, leafy greens, and fortified cereals. Supplements may be necessary if dietary intake is insufficient.

Hydration

Older adults are at increased risk of dehydration. Drink water regularly even if you don't feel thirsty. Herbal teas, soups, and water-rich fruits like watermelon and cucumbers also contribute to hydration.

Limit Sugar and Sodium

Too much sugar and sodium can increase the risk of chronic diseases. Opt for natural sweeteners and use herbs and spices to flavour foods instead of salt.

2. Physical Activity: Movement for Mobility and Vitality

Staying active is one of the most important ways to maintain health and independence in later life. Exercise can prevent or manage many chronic conditions and improve balance, flexibility, and mood.

Recommended Activities

- **Aerobic Exercise**: Aim for at least 150 minutes of moderate-intensity aerobic activity per week. Activities include brisk walking, swimming, cycling, or dancing.
- **Strength Training**: Engage in muscle-strengthening activities at least twice a week. Use resistance bands, light weights, or body-weight exercises.
- **Flexibility and Balance**: Incorporate stretching, yoga, or tai chi to improve flexibility and reduce the risk of falls.
- **Daily Movement**: Gardening, housework, and leisurely strolls also count. The goal is to keep moving and avoid long periods of sedentary behaviour.

Safety Tips

- Consult your healthcare provider before starting a new exercise regimen.
- Use proper footwear and consider supportive equipment if needed.
- Start slow and build intensity gradually.

3. Mental and Emotional Health: Nurturing Inner Wellness

Emotional well-being is just as important as physical health. As people age, they may experience life changes such as retirement, loss of loved ones, or decreased mobility, which can impact mental health.

Staying Mentally Active

- **Lifelong Learning**: Take a class, learn a new language, or explore a musical instrument.
- **Puzzles and Games**: Crossword puzzles, Sudoku, and board games help stimulate the brain.
- **Reading and Writing**: Books, journaling, and storytelling can sharpen cognitive skills.
- **Technology**: Embrace new tools and platforms to stay connected and informed.

Emotional Resilience

- **Stay Connected**: Engage regularly with family, friends, and community.
- **Mindfulness and Meditation**: Practice techniques to manage stress and promote emotional balance.
- **Seek Help When Needed**: Don't hesitate to talk to a therapist or counsellor. Depression and anxiety are treatable at any age.
- **Spiritual Engagement**: Whether through religion, nature, or personal beliefs, spiritual practices can provide comfort and meaning.

4. Preventative Healthcare: Staying Ahead of Illness

Preventative healthcare focuses on avoiding illness or detecting it early when it is most treatable.

Regular Screenings and Exams

- **Annual Check-ups**: Visit your healthcare provider yearly for a comprehensive physical.
- **Vision and Hearing Tests**: Regular exams can identify issues that impact quality of life and safety.
- **Dental Health**: See a dentist at least once a year. Oral health is linked to heart disease and diabetes.
- **Bone Density Scans**: Monitor for osteoporosis, especially in women over 65.

Vaccinations

- Stay up to date on recommended vaccines, including:
    - Flu Shot (yearly)
    - Shingles Vaccine
    - Pneumococcal Vaccine
    - COVID-19 Vaccine and Boosters

Medication Management

- Review prescriptions regularly with your doctor.
- Be aware of potential interactions and side effects.
- Use pill organisers or digital reminders.

5. Sleep: Restorative Health from Rest

Quality sleep is vital for memory, mood, and physical health. Many older adults experience changes in sleep patterns, but it's important to aim for 7-8 hours of quality sleep each night.

Tips for Better Sleep

- Maintain a regular sleep schedule.
- Create a relaxing bedtime routine.
- Limit screen time before bed.
- Avoid caffeine and large meals late in the day.
- Keep your bedroom dark, quiet, and cool.

6. Fall Prevention: Protecting Independence

Falls are a leading cause of injury among seniors. Preventing falls means maintaining independence and avoiding unnecessary hospital visits.

Fall-Proofing Your Home

- Remove tripping hazards like loose rugs or clutter.
- Install grab bars in bathrooms and handrails on stairs.
- Ensure adequate lighting throughout your home.
- Use non-slip mats in the bathtub and shower.

Strength and Balance Training

- Engage in exercises that improve coordination.
- Consider physical therapy if you feel unsteady.
- Have your vision checked and wear supportive footwear.

7. Social Engagement: Health Through Connection

Social connection plays a vital role in overall well-being. Isolation can lead to depression, cognitive decline, and physical health problems.

Ways to Stay Socially Active

- Join community or senior centres.

- Volunteer for causes you care about.
- Schedule regular get-togethers with friends and family.
- Use technology to connect with distant loved ones.

8. Financial Wellness: Peace of Mind for Healthy Living

Financial stress can negatively impact health. Managing your finances can help reduce anxiety and support healthy lifestyle choices.

Tips for Financial Health

- Create a budget and track expenses.
- Meet with a financial planner if needed.
- Take advantage of senior discounts and benefits.
- Plan for long-term care, including insurance options.

9. Purpose and Meaning: The Heart of Healthy Living

A sense of purpose is linked to better health outcomes and longer life. Retirement is an opportunity to redefine your purpose.

Finding Your Why

- Volunteer for a cause that resonates with you.
- Mentor younger generations.
- Explore creative pursuits like writing, painting, or music.
- Set personal goals, no matter how small.

Real-Life Inspirations

John, 72 – The Marathon Walker After retirement, John took up daily walks. He now logs over 10,000 steps a day and participates in charity walking events. Walking keeps him fit and has introduced him to a new circle of friends.

Maria, 68 – The Community Chef Maria started a community cooking class for seniors focused on heart-healthy meals. She shares recipes, teaches skills, and has created a network of like-minded health enthusiasts.

Ben and Claire, 75 and 74 – The Traveling Duo Ben and Claire make a point to travel to a new location every year. They prepare by staying active, eating healthy, and scheduling checkups before every trip. Their shared adventures fuel both their physical health and their emotional connection.

Conclusion

Staying healthy in your senior years is not about perfection, it's about progress and proactive living. Every step you take toward better health counts. By eating well, staying active, prioritising mental and emotional well-being, and engaging with your community, you can build a lifestyle that supports longevity and joy.

Health in retirement is a journey, not a destination. It requires mindfulness, adaptability, and a willingness to embrace change. With the right habits, resources, and mindset, you can age not just gracefully, but vibrantly.

In the next chapter, we'll explore how to create a safe and accessible home environment that supports independence and comfort throughout the aging process.

Creating a Safe Home

Aging brings with it new priorities, and among the most important is the need for a home that supports safety, comfort, and independence. As people grow older, their physical abilities may change, and so must the spaces they inhabit. Creating a safe and accessible home environment is more than just making a few renovations, it's about reimagining your space as a long-term sanctuary, one that grows with you. This chapter will explore how to thoughtfully adapt your home to meet the evolving needs of aging, ensuring it remains a haven of dignity, warmth, and freedom.

The Importance of Aging in Place

Aging in place refers to the ability to live in your own home safely, independently, and comfortably, regardless of age or ability level. According to AARP, nearly 90% of adults over 65 want to remain in their current home and community as they age. The reasons are deeply personal, emotional attachment, familiarity, and community connections all play a role.

Remaining at home can support emotional well-being, reduce the costs of institutional care, and preserve autonomy. However, to successfully age in place, homes must be thoughtfully adapted to minimise risk and enhance function.

Assessing Your Current Living Space

The first step toward creating a supportive home is assessment. Walk through each room with a critical eye, preferably with a checklist or professional home assessment guide. Key things to look for include:

- Tripping hazards like rugs, cords, and uneven flooring
- Poor lighting or shadows that obscure walkways
- Hard-to-reach cabinets or shelves
- Narrow doorways or halls that might not accommodate mobility aids
- Bathroom risks, such as slippery tubs and lack of grab bars

You may wish to involve an occupational therapist or certified aging-in-place specialist (CAPS) to perform a more in-depth analysis. They can recommend specific improvements tailored to your abilities and lifestyle.

Key Principles of a Senior-Friendly Home

When modifying your home, consider the following principles that form the foundation of universal design, an approach that makes spaces usable by all people, regardless of age or ability.

1. **Safety**: Minimise risks of falls, burns, and other injuries.
2. **Accessibility**: Ensure ease of entry and movement throughout the house.
3. **Comfort**: Promote ease of use and restful, stress-free living.

4. **Independence**: Empower the ability to perform daily tasks without assistance.
5. **Adaptability**: Choose flexible designs that can accommodate future needs.

Room-by-Room Guide to Home Modifications

Let's explore specific changes you can make, room by room, to enhance the safety and comfort of your home.

1. Entryways and Exterior

- **Install ramps** or no-step entries to replace stairs.
- **Widen doorways** to at least 36 inches to accommodate wheelchairs and walkers.
- **Add handrails** on both sides of exterior steps.
- **Ensure proper lighting** with motion-sensor or dusk-to-dawn exterior lights.
- **Secure entry mats** or use slip-resistant surfaces.
- **Install a peephole or smart doorbell** to enhance security.

2. Living Room

- **Arrange furniture** to create clear walkways (at least 36 inches wide).
- **Remove or tape down rugs** to prevent tripping.
- **Use chairs with armrests** and firm cushions to aid standing.
- **Add task lighting** next to seating areas.
- **Install lever-style door handles** and light switches for easier grip.

3. Kitchen

- **Place frequently used items** within easy reach (between knee and shoulder height).
- **Use D-shaped cabinet handles** instead of knobs.
- **Install pull-out shelves** or lazy Susans in cabinets.
- **Consider a wall oven and side-opening microwave** to reduce bending and lifting.
- **Use an anti-scald device** on the kitchen sink.
- **Ensure flooring is non-slip** and easy to clean.

4. Bathroom

- **Install grab bars** near the toilet and in the shower/tub.
- **Use a walk-in shower** with a bench and handheld showerhead.
- **Apply non-slip mats or strips** inside and outside the tub.
- **Raise the toilet seat** or install a comfort-height toilet.
- **Add a nightlight** or motion-sensor lighting.
- **Keep toiletries organised** and within easy reach.

5. Bedroom

- **Choose a bed of proper height** for easy entry and exit.
- **Place a phone and flashlight** within arm's reach of the bed.
- **Use touch-activated or remote-controlled lights**.
- **Ensure closet rods and drawers** are easily accessible.

- **Add grab bars or handrails**, if needed, for getting in and out of bed.

6. Hallways and Stairs

- **Install handrails on both sides** of staircases.
- **Apply non-slip stair treads** or carpeting.
- **Ensure consistent lighting**, especially at the top and bottom of stairs.
- **Use contrasting colours** on stair edges to improve visibility.

General Safety Upgrades

- **Smoke and Carbon Monoxide Detectors**: Install in every bedroom and common area; test monthly.
- **Medical Alert Systems**: Consider wearable alert devices for emergencies.
- **Smart Home Devices**: Use voice-activated assistants, smart thermostats, and remote monitoring tools.
- **Flooring**: Choose low-pile carpet or smooth, non-slip surfaces like cork or vinyl.
- **Eliminate Clutter**: Clear pathways and minimise decorative obstacles.

Our Story – Preparing for later

As we approached our own retirement, we realised that making my home more adaptable to the changes ahead was essential for maintaining independence and comfort. One of the first steps we took was to move to a new home with fewer steps, eliminating the daily struggle of climbing stairs. We chose a home where there were no outside steps to navigate as we entered.

Additionally, we focused on refurbishing the basement to create a fully functional apartment. This would be a perfect solution for when navigating upstairs becomes more difficult. The space was transformed into a cosy, accessible living area with wide doorways, an easily accessible bathroom, and everything on one level. It's reassuring to know that we've set the foundation for a smooth transition, ensuring that as we enter our later retirement, we can do so with a sense of security, autonomy, and peace of mind in a home that grows with us.

Technology for Aging in Place

Modern technology offers powerful tools to enhance independence and safety at home:

- **Voice Assistants** (Amazon Alexa, Google Home): Set reminders, make calls, control lights.
- **Video Doorbells and Cameras**: Increase home security and visibility.
- **Medication Dispensers**: Automated pill reminders to support health routines.
- **Motion Sensors**: Alert caregivers to inactivity or falls.
- **Telehealth Systems**: Virtual doctor visits and remote monitoring tools reduce the need to travel.

Emotional and Psychological Comfort

A safe home isn't just physically secure; it should also nurture emotional well-being:

- **Personalise your space** with photos, favourite art, and familiar furniture.
- **Include indoor plants** or garden views to enhance calm and joy.
- **Create cosy zones** for reading, hobbies, or music.
- **Keep social spaces** like the dining or living room inviting for guests and gatherings.

Planning for Future Needs

As aging progresses, your needs may evolve. Plan for potential changes:

- **Install blocking in walls** during renovations for future grab bar placement.
- **Ensure bathroom floors are waterproof** in case of assisted bathing later on.
- **Choose flexible furniture** that can be rearranged as mobility changes.
- **Locate your bedroom on the main floor** to reduce reliance on stairs.
- **Prepare a care plan** that includes emergency contacts, medication lists, and medical records.

When to Consider Professional Help

Creating an age-friendly home can be complex. Don't hesitate to bring in professionals:

- **Certified Aging-in-Place Specialists (CAPS)**: Trained in design and remodelling for senior needs.
- **Occupational Therapists**: Assess mobility and recommend custom adaptations.

- **Home Health Providers**: Evaluate the home environment from a caregiving standpoint.
- **Contractors and Builders**: Ensure all modifications meet safety and building codes.

Financial Assistance and Resources

Adapting your home doesn't have to break the bank. Explore the following options:

- **Medicare and Medicaid**: May cover some durable medical equipment (e.g., grab bars, hospital beds).
- **Veterans Benefits**: Programs like HISA (Home Improvements and Structural Alterations) grants.
- **State and Local Agencies**: Area Agencies on Aging often offer grants or referrals.
- **Nonprofits**: Rebuilding Together, Habitat for Humanity, and others may assist with home repairs.
- **Tax Deductions**: Certain home improvements may qualify as medical expenses.

Real-Life Examples

Edna, 76 – The Early Planner After seeing her sister struggle with mobility, Edna decided to renovate her bathroom to include a zero-threshold shower and non-slip tiles. She also installed brighter lighting and lowered her kitchen cabinets. Now she lives confidently and independently in her home of 40 years.

James, 81 – The Tech-Savvy Senior James integrated smart technology throughout his home, voice-activated lights, automated blinds, and a medical alert bracelet linked to emergency services. With arthritis affecting his hands, he replaced all doorknobs with levers and added a bidet with remote controls.

Sofia, 88 – The Garden Guardian Sofia loved her garden but was nervous about the uneven paths. Her family installed level walkways, raised beds, and sturdy benches, allowing her to continue her hobby with ease. Her garden now doubles as a social space, where neighbours gather for tea.

Home as a Source of Empowerment

Your home should be your partner in aging, a space that supports your health, reflects your personality, and evolves with you. The process of adapting your home isn't just about avoiding accidents; it's about enhancing your quality of life.

A well-designed environment fosters autonomy, nurtures confidence, and provides a foundation for joyful, independent living. With the right planning and support, you can create a home that's not only safe but deeply satisfying for the decades ahead.

In the next chapter, we'll explore the importance of staying mentally engaged through hobbies, learning, and creative pursuits that keep your mind sharp and your spirit young.

Start Today

"The best time to plant a tree was 20 years ago. The second-best time is now." – Chinese Proverb

As a recent retiree, one of the most common sentiments I encounter from others is this: "I wish I had started earlier." That one phrase carries a universe of meaning. It is at once a confession, a regret, and a realisation. It acknowledges the critical role of time in the success of retirement planning, while also highlighting one of the most pervasive human tendencies: procrastination.

Understanding the Cost of Delay

To grasp the significance of starting today, we must first understand the cost of delay. Retirement planning is not a one-time event. It is a process that evolves over decades and impacts nearly every aspect of your life. The longer you delay, the more compressed your window becomes for achieving financial security, developing personal interests, and preparing for the psychological shift that retirement entails.

Financial Consequences

The most measurable consequence of procrastination is financial. Consider the principle of compound interest, a foundational concept in personal finance. Time allows your investments to grow exponentially. For example, if you begin saving $500 per month at age 30 with an average return of 6% per year, by the time you reach 65, you will have approximately $760,000. If you wait until age 40 to begin, that amount drops to around $392,000. Waiting until age 50? Just $182,000. The numbers are staggering.

But beyond investment returns, delaying planning means potentially missing out on employer-matching contributions to retirement accounts, delaying debt reduction efforts, and being forced to contribute significantly more per month later in life to make up for lost time. This often results in increased financial stress during a period of life that should be defined by freedom and fulfilment.

Psychological and Emotional Costs

The consequences of delay are not just financial. Retirement is a profound psychological transition – from career identity to personal reinvention. The earlier you begin thinking about what retirement means for you, the more equipped you will be to handle that change. Many retirees struggle with feelings of loss, boredom, or purposelessness after leaving the workforce. These challenges are easier to address when you have taken time to develop hobbies, cultivate relationships, and explore new passions in advance.

Delaying these explorations can lead to emotional unpreparedness, anxiety, and even depression in retirement. Planning your lifestyle today allows you to ease into new roles and interests gradually, rather than being forced to reinvent yourself overnight.

Why Do We Delay

Despite the clear benefits of starting early, most people still delay. Why? The reasons are many and varied, but they often fall into a few broad categories:

1. **Overwhelm:** The topic of retirement planning can be intimidating. Investments, taxes, insurance, estate planning – the complexity can be paralysing. Many people feel they lack the knowledge to begin and are afraid of making costly mistakes.
2. **Disconnection from Future Self:** Psychologists have found that people often see their future selves as strangers. This cognitive disconnect leads us to prioritise short-term gratification over long-term planning.
3. **Competing Priorities:** Life is busy. Raising children, paying off student loans, caring for aging parents – retirement planning often takes a back seat to more immediate concerns.
4. **Fear:** Thinking about retirement forces us to confront aging, mortality, and financial insecurity. For some, it is easier to avoid the topic altogether than to face these uncomfortable realities.

Understanding these psychological barriers is the first step in overcoming them. The next step is to reframe the narrative: planning for retirement is not an exercise in fear or sacrifice – it is an act of empowerment and self-care.

The Benefits of Starting Today

When you treat today as the starting line, you immediately shift from a reactive mindset to a proactive one. The benefits are both tangible and intangible.

Financial Clarity and Momentum

Starting today allows you to assess your current financial position and begin creating a realistic plan for the future. You gain clarity on your income, expenses, savings rate, and investment options. This clarity fosters momentum. Even small steps, setting up automatic transfers to a retirement account, increasing contributions by 1%, meeting with a financial advisor, build over time.

This momentum can be self-reinforcing. As you begin to see progress, your confidence grows. You become more engaged, more informed, and more intentional with your financial decisions.

Psychological Readiness

Planning today also prepares you mentally and emotionally for the retirement transition. It gives you time to consider critical questions: Who am I without my job? What will give me purpose in retirement? How will I structure my days? Will I volunteer, travel, start a business, pursue creative passions?

When you start thinking about these questions early, you create space to experiment and explore. You can test out new hobbies, build social connections outside of work, and begin shaping a retirement lifestyle that is meaningful and fulfilling.

Health and Lifestyle Benefits

One often overlooked aspect of retirement planning is health. Starting today means making intentional choices to preserve your health for the long term. This includes diet, exercise, stress management, and preventive care. Poor health is one of the most common obstacles to enjoying retirement.

If you begin today with small, sustainable changes, walking daily, preparing nutritious meals, quitting smoking, managing sleep, you significantly increase your chances of remaining active and independent in your later years.

Simple Steps to Start Now

Starting today doesn't require a complete overhaul. In fact, the most effective changes are often the simplest. Here are practical, manageable steps you can take today:

1. **Set a Retirement Vision:** Write down what you want your retirement to look like. Where will you live? How will you spend your time? Who will you spend it with?
2. **Assess Your Finances:** Take stock of your assets, liabilities, income, and expenses. Use this as a baseline to determine how much you need to save.
3. **Open or Maximise Retirement Accounts:** If you haven't already, open an IRA or contribute more to your employer-sponsored plan. Take full advantage of any employer match.
4. **Automate Your Savings:** Set up automatic transfers to your retirement account. Even small contributions add up over time.
5. **Start a Health Habit:** Begin with something small but consistent, a 10-minute walk, a healthy lunch swap, or a daily stretch routine.

6. **Educate Yourself:** Read a book on retirement planning, listen to a financial podcast, or attend a local seminar.
7. **Talk to Someone:** Discuss your retirement goals with a partner, friend, or financial advisor. Making it social makes it real.

These steps are not just about action; they are about identity. Each one signals a shift in how you see yourself: from someone who is avoiding retirement planning to someone who is actively shaping the future.

Case Studies: The Difference a Day Makes

To illustrate the power of starting today, consider the following simplified case studies:

Case Study 1: Starting at 30 Sarah begins contributing $400 per month to her retirement account at age 30. She earns an average return of 6% per year. By the time she is 65, her account is worth approximately $635,000.

Case Study 2: Starting at 45 James waits until age 45 to begin. He contributes the same $400 per month. By 65, he accumulates only about $204,000.

Difference: One decision to start earlier results in an additional $431,000 in retirement savings. This is not due to larger contributions, but to time. Sarah gave her money more years to grow.

Now apply this principle beyond finances. Consider emotional readiness. Consider health. Consider social connection. In every domain, starting today widens your options and increases your likelihood of success.

The Emotional Shift of Commitment

Something transformative happens when you commit to starting today. You begin to shift from a sense of scarcity to a sense of agency. Retirement planning no longer feels like a looming threat; it becomes a hopeful, creative, and strategic process. You begin to realise that retirement is not the end of something. It is the beginning of something new.

You also start to reclaim power over your time. One of the great ironies is that people often delay planning for retirement because they feel they don't have time, yet the very act of planning is what allows you to free your time later.

Our Story – Why We Retired

As I mentioned earlier in the book, our retirement journey began not by careful planning or a grand announcement, but by a reshuffle at the company I had worked for most of my life. At the time, it felt abrupt, almost like the rug had been pulled out from under me. But looking back now, I see it clearly for what it was: a gift in disguise. That reshuffle, unintended by the company, changed my life, for the better.

Since retiring, my days have taken on a new shape, one defined not by deadlines or office politics, but by freedom. I've taken up hobbies I never had time for, booked vacations to places I once only dreamed of, and learned how to live with intention rather than obligation. There are no more emails demanding my attention after hours. No more meetings filled with empty buzzwords. No more pretending to agree with a manager who believed they knew how to the tasks better than me, simply because that's what was expected.

> Now, I choose how I spend my time, what I focus on, and what I believe is worth pursuing.
>
> Life in retirement isn't empty, it's full. Full of opportunities, exploration, quiet mornings, meaningful conversations, and laughter that isn't rushed. It's a second chapter, written entirely on your own terms.
>
> So now, I turn the question to you. Where are you in your story? Is it time to start imagining what your life could look like without the constraints of a nine-to-five? Retirement doesn't mean stopping, it means shifting toward a life built around what truly matters to you.
>
> Don't wait for a company reshuffle to push you into the next chapter. Take the pen in your own hand. Plan your retirement. Make it real. You won't regret it.

Overcoming Perfectionism

One final barrier to starting today is perfectionism. Many people hesitate to begin because they feel they need all the answers first. They want the perfect budget, the perfect plan, the perfect moment.

Here's the truth: Perfection is the enemy of progress. You will never have all the answers. Your first plan will not be your last. But every step you take today makes the next step easier. The best retirement plans are living documents. They evolve. But they must begin.

Today is the Day

If there is one message to carry from this book it is this: Start today. Not next week. Not after the next vacation. Not once you get that raise or pay off that credit card. Start now. Even if all you do is make one phone call, write one goal, or transfer $50 to your retirement account – you have begun.

Time is your greatest ally when it comes to retirement planning. But only if you use it. Each day you delay, your options narrow. Each day you take action, they expand.

You owe it to your future self to begin now. You deserve the peace of mind that comes from knowing you are on your way. Retirement is not a finish line; it is a new chapter. And today is page one.

Your Action Step: Right now, write down one thing you can do today to begin your retirement journey. Then do it. Today. Your future self will thank you.

Thank You

If you found this book helpful, leaving a review on Amazon or your preferred platform makes a big difference. Your feedback helps other readers discover valuable guidance, supports independent authors, and encourages more content like this. Whether it's a quick note or a detailed comment, your words matter, and they help others make informed decisions on their retirement journey. Thank you for taking a moment to share your thoughts, it truly means a lot.

Steven

www.ingramcontent.com/pod-product-compliance
Lightning Source LLC
Chambersburg PA
CBHW071438230926
51846CB00001B/274
* 9 7 8 1 9 8 9 6 8 1 4 5 9 *